Carsten Bothe

LEATHER SEWING

8 New Projects for Leather Crafters of All Levels

SCHIFFER
PUBLISHING

4880 Lower Valley Road • Atglen, PA 19310

Originally published as *Leder nähen: Neue Projekte* © 2020 HEEL Verlag GmbH
Translated from the German by Simulingua, Inc.

Library of Congress Control Number: 2022932579

Cover design by Molly Shields
Photographs: © Carsten Bothe, with the exception of: © stock.adobe.com: NorGal (Cover 1 a), Eky Chan (Cover 1 c), Iricat (Cover 1 round leather), simone_n (Cover 1 b), 123creative (Cover 4 background), emevil (pp. 4–5), Sven Käppler (p. 30)
Type set in Adelle

ISBN: 978-0-7643-6499-0
Printed in India

Published by Schiffer Publishing, Ltd.
4880 Lower Valley Road
Atglen, PA 19310
Phone: (610) 593-1777; Fax: (610) 593-2002
Email: Info@schifferbooks.com
Web: www.schifferbooks.com

For our complete selection of fine books on this and related subjects, please visit our website at www.schifferbooks.com. You may also write for a free catalog.

Schiffer Publishing's titles are available at special discounts for bulk purchases for sales promotions or premiums. Special editions, including personalized covers, corporate imprints, and excerpts, can be created in large quantities for special needs. For more information, contact the publisher.

We are always looking for people to write books on new and related subjects. If you have an idea for a book, please contact us at proposals@schifferbooks.com.

Note
To make the text easier to read, we have decided to describe how to do the work by someone who is right-handed. Anyone who is left-handed should work the other way around.

Other Schiffer Books by the Author:
Practical Leatherwork: Cutting, Sewing, Finishing & Repair, ISBN 978-0-7643-5744-2

Other Schiffer Books on Related Subjects:
Leathercraft: Traditional Hand-crafted Leatherwork Skills and Projects, Nigel Armitage, ISBN 978-0-7643-6039-8

Quilted Leather: Adding Texture, Dimension, and Style to Leather Crafting, Cathy Wiggins, ISBN 978-0-7643-5500-4

Little Delights in Leather: Charming Projects to Use Every Day, Mélanie Voituriez, ISBN 978-0-7643-5838-8

Dear Reader,

Sewing leather is a craft that is becoming more and more popular and is a hobby that you can start without any big expenditure or investment. Besides, it is fun. You are creating something individual, and also it doesn't make a mess. You can make individual, durable, and sustainable leather products at home on your kitchen.

Anyone who is already experienced in working with leather will find further suggestions in this book, and beginners will find good instructions for getting started in the "Simple Projects" category. At the same time, this doesn't so much involve re-creating a project that is presented one to one, but rather using it to orient yourself and create something of your own. Therefore, the methods used are described precisely for each project. Making the apron, for example, doesn't involve exactly replicating the steps that I present; rather, I want to show you how to develop your own pattern and why you construct something in a particular way and not a different way. With this knowledge, you can then work creatively and will be able to call a custom-made apron your own.

I wish you a lot of success and fun handcrafting your leather projects and look forward to feedback or questions, which I would be happy to receive from you at info@carstenbothe.de.

Cordially yours,

Carsten Bothe

Table of Contents

First Steps—Tools

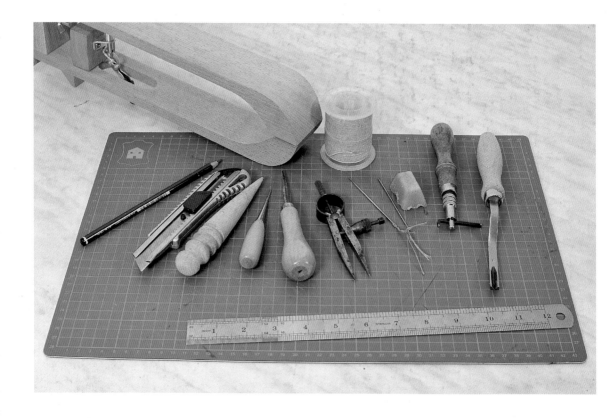

With just these few tools, you can already achieve some impressive leather projects.

You need a certain number of tools for professional leather sewing. But with an awl, two needles, a spool of thread, and a sharp cutter, you are already well equipped for hobby-level work and you can improvise everything else. For example, you can clamp the leather in a vise for sewing, mark the seams with the compass, and use the handle of a tool to burnish the edges. The results will become better and more professional if you gradually buy specialized work equipment. In the following pages, you will find an overview of the most commonly used tools.

Workplace

The beauty of sewing leather is that it hardly makes any mess and no noise at all, so you could even simply use your kitchen table as a workplace. When working, however, you will always need sufficient diffuse light, coming from all directions. This is especially important when tooling the leather, because a hand or a tool will always be throwing a shadow where you work. The table should be stable and provide enough space to spread out even a large hide if you want to lay out patterns or cut off straps.

Cutting Mat

You will cut many things out on a cutting mat. Therefore, a large handicraft work surface is essential. "Self-healing" cutting mats work the best; these also absorb deep cuts while leaving a smooth surface and dampen impact noises. In a pinch, you can use a cutting board from the kitchen at first. To prevent the board from slipping, an antislip mat underneath helps; you can also use it for other applications while working with leather.

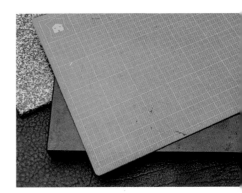

Stone Slab

For tooling, you need a solid foundation that provides support when using the stamping or other tools. The leather gets compressed between this foundation and the stamping tool. Therefore, the foundation must not be something that will give way under any circumstances. Polished stone slabs have proven themselves, and with a little luck, you can acquire one inexpensively. I myself use a slab made from an old "hot stone," but pieces from marble window sills also work well. The slab must be polished to a mirror finish and have an even surface, so it doesn't leave any impressions on the leather. The weight is also decisive, because the heavier and bigger the slab is, the better you can work on it. For this, of course, you need a solid table that will neither wobble nor cave in. The larger the stone slab, the thicker it has to be so that it will not break apart. You should put an antislip mat under the slab. For thinner slabs in particular, make sure that they always lie flush to the table, with no hollows beneath, or otherwise they may break apart.

Knives

For professionals, there are the expensive half-moon knives—also called round knives—but it is necessary to practice using them. Cobbler's knives sharpened on one side with a beveled cutting edge are the more attractive option for your wallet. The disadvantage of these knives, however, is that you have to sharpen them yourself—which isn't easy. For beginners, simple cutters with breakaway blades are ideal and unbeatably cheap.

Awls

Without awls, nothing works in sewing leather. You need two types: for one, a sharply polished diamond awl with a diamond-shaped cross section and sharp sides, and for the other, a round awl. You use the latter to widen the holes if you want to sew two stitches to finish a seam without running the risk of cutting the thread, which happens all too easily when you use a diamond awl.

The diamond awl should have a handle with flat sides so that you can intuitively feel the position of the awl and especially of the sharp cutting edges. You should also polish the awl to a mirror-like finish, but do not make the point needle-sharp. Instead, round it off to a width of 1 millimeter (0.04 inches) on the front and polish until sharp. This makes it easier to guide it in the leather. The round awl can have a round handle; here, the alignment doesn't matter.

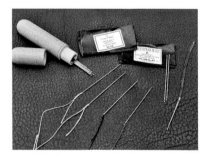

Needles

Needles that work well for sewing leather should have a round, blunt point so that you don't prick yourself and also won't pierce the other thread that easily. So that you don't lose your needles, you can always leave the rest of the thread in the needle until you have prepared a new thread. Alternatively, you can simply stick the needles into the beeswax block in the meantime (see p. 11).

Thread

There are basically two types of threads: natural threads made of flax, cotton, or hemp, and threads made of synthetics. Personally, I use only natural materials, because that is what feels good, and for me, it just fits better with the natural leather material. Natural threads are difficult to work with when using a machine. This is due to the fact that the thread varies in how thick and rough it is, which makes no difference when sewing by hand. One advantage of twisted natural threads is that they are easier to bring to a point and thread into the needle. The threads are twisted together from several strands and can be easily untwisted when threading, so that they go through the needle eye. The choice of colors is rather limited. There is little more available besides black, white, and natural-colored thread.

Threads made of synthetics—but also some types made of cotton—are not twisted, but braided. These are called "Forellenfaden" ("trout thread") in Germany. You cannot unbraid or untwist these threads between your fingers. Depending on the manufacturer, these threads are already waxed and therefore ready for sewing. Thread made of polyester comes in all the colors of the rainbow, so it is ideal for decorative seams.

You can secure synthetic threads quite easily by sewing back two stitches; sew one more stitch with the thread on the visible side and then trim the threads to 5 mm (0.2 inches) on the back of the piece. Then melt this remaining 5 mm (0.2 inches) of thread with a lighter into a ball, which will securely keep the seam from coming loose.

The threads should be 0.7 to 1 mm (0.03 to 0.04 inches) thick—for leather that is 4 mm (0.16 inches) thick, this is a good ratio of thread and leather thickness. A thread that is too thin cuts into the leather and doesn't hold properly; a thread that is too thick needs holes that are too large, which weakens the leather.

Wooden Leather Creaser and Edge Beveler

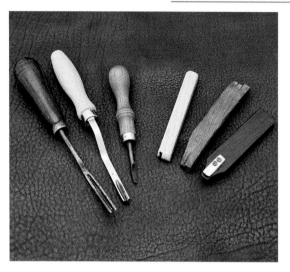

Next to the upper surface of the leather, a piece also makes an impact by clean workmanship along the edge. To bring an edge that has been cut at right angles to the surface into shape, you should first cut a decorative groove in the grain side, using a leather creaser. There are several tools for doing this, from a metal design to specially cut and polished pieces of wood, to tools with bone inserts. But they always function in the same way: One part keeps it at the same distance from the edge; to do this, you guide the tool along the edge so that the guide arm aligns neatly. The other part cuts the groove. When dropping in this line, the important thing is to first work using little pressure and then work your way forward step by step and, at the same time, gradually increase the pressure, until the depth and color come out as desired.

Use the edge beveler to bevel the edge; you do this by cutting off a part of the leather at a 45-degree angle. You should select the edge beveler so that it will remove about ¼ of the thickness of the leather on both the grain and flesh side each time. A range of edge bevelers in different widths is available in stores.

Wooden Leather Burnisher and Bone Folder

To burnish the edges of the leather, you will need a wooden leather burnisher. This is a round tool with grooves of different widths machined into it. You stroke these grooves along the edge, and then with force and speed, you round off and burnish the edge.

Alternatively, you can use a folder made of bone. The work is a little more difficult using this tool, but also possible. One advantage is that you can use the tip of the bone folder to draw lines on the grain side of the leather and use the round side to "rub them out" again.

Stitching Pony

To sew leather safely and precisely, a stitching clamp—also called a stitching pony—is absolutely necessary. Many of the leather dealers on the internet have these clamps available for the hobby lea-ther crafter. It's important that you fasten this tool on securely and solidly to the work surface, using two screw clamps. You can upgrade simple models by attaching a thin piece of leather to the clamping jaws.

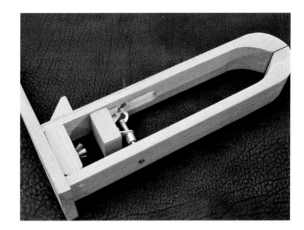

Other

A metal ruler is helpful for drawing and also cutting along straight lines. If the ruler slips too much on the leather, you can simply cover the underside with fine sandpaper.

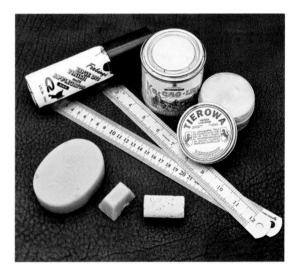

You should stock up on some corks to protect the awls when you transport them. You can also use the corks to protect your hands if the awl won't slip easily through thick leather. To do this, hold a cork against the piece from the other side, and as the tip of the awl emerges, it will stick only into the cork and not into your finger.

To prepare a natural thread, you need a block of beeswax. A block the size of a bar of soap will be enough. You can also rub the wax into the edges of the leather and thus burnish them.

If you want to dye the edge, you need edge dye. This comes with an applicator, which makes applying the dye quick and clean work, or in small canisters, so that you will need a large cotton swab to extract the dye. Edge dye is hard to get out of textiles, and you should be very careful not to knock these small containers over onto the work surface. You can fill a shallow bowl with sand and push the dye container into it. That will prevent the worst from happening.

After it is finished, you should protect your piece. Many different kinds of leather oils, dubbing wax (leather conditioner), or other commercial leather care products are available on the market. However, these differ in how they make the leather darken. You should test the product on a remnant before-hand to see whether you are satisfied with the result, because if it should turn out too dark, you cannot correct it anymore.

Types of Leather

There are huge differences in the way leather is tanned. Most leather in the world is tanned for industrial processing. For the most part, this involves inferior hides that have been tanned using chemical substances. They are usually so thin that it would not be possible to apply a reasonable hand seam. As a result, this leather is not suitable for the projects described in this book.

In essence, you will need the following kinds of leather for the projects.

Oil-Tanned / Saddle Leather

Oil-tanned or saddle leather is a thick cowhide that has been vegetable-tanned first and is practically ready to use; it does not need any oiling or waxing or surface treatment later on. You will need it when you want to make a simple belt or pair of suspenders. This leather is difficult to tool, and instead it is mostly used as is.

Chrome-Tanned Leather

Chrome-tanned leather is a very hard-wearing type of leather that can also be finished with other features, such as a water-repellent coating. It is used as upholstery leather or for sturdy aprons. The leather apron in this book is made of chrome leather because it falls softly and it is easy to wipe stains off.

Vegetable-Tanned Leather

Vegetable-tanned or "veg tan" leather, also called russet leather, is basically the same leather as oil-tanned leather. The difference is that it is still untreated and natural. That is why it soaks up water like a sponge, which is necessary for tooling work. This leather also lends itself to being dyed with water-based leather dyes or stains. However, vegetable-tanned leather is very sensitive and becomes discolored if it is exposed to the sun without protection. You can use this leather to make anything that you can also make when using oil-tanned leather. The advantage lies in the option to dye or tool it. When you do this, you subsequently have to make it water repellent by applying leather oil or wax or other care products. At the same time, this will make the leather darker, more or less, depending on the product used, so you should definitely test the care product on a remnant beforehand.

Chamois Leather

Chamois leather involves using the oldest type of finishing. The surface is the same on both the grain and flesh side, and it is popular for making clothing, such as Bavarian lederhosen. It is actually white to slightly yellow but can be dyed on one side by applying brushed-on dye. It is very soft and falls more like a heavy fabric. Chamois does not have the stiffness that other types of leather do.

Sewing Techniques

"A good seam holds as long as the leather itself."

Sewing leather is the classic way to join two pieces of leather together. Gluing and riveting were added on only later to save production costs. You can already make a professional-looking and durable saddler's seam with a few tools and a little practice. The following describes a selection of seams and techniques that will help you achieve success quickly.

Saddle Stitch—Join Two Overlapping Pieces of Leather

To join two pieces of leather, you use the so-called saddle stitch. To do this, you work using two needles; one is looped onto each end of a piece of thread. Treating it with beeswax and pitch, if necessary, makes the thread even more durable. It sticks in the seam holes so that the seam will not come undone even if part of the thread should become frayed through or unraveled.

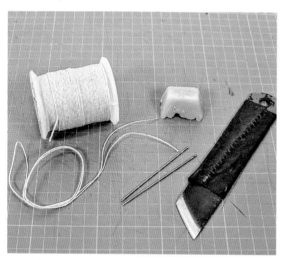

Preparing the needle and thread: thread, two needles, beeswax, and knife

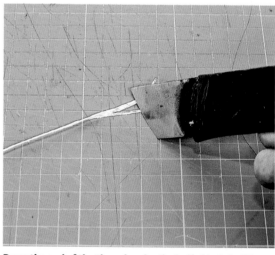

Draw the end of the thread under the knife blade to thin out the thread and bring it to a point.

Here you can see the scraped fibers and the thinned-out thread.

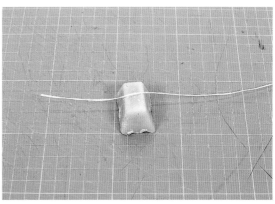

Pull the thread and especially the ends through the block of beeswax.

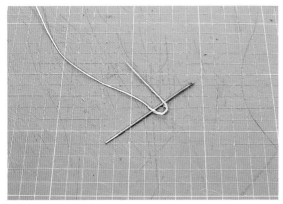

Starting from the end, stick the needle through the thread twice.

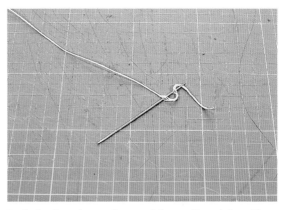

Push the thread up to the eye of the needle and thread it through the eye.

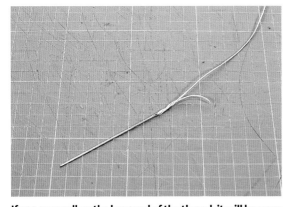

If you now pull on the long end of the thread, it will become twisted around so that it cannot slip out of the eye again.

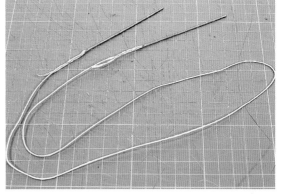

Both ends of the thread are threaded through the needles.

Before starting to sew, you have to join both pieces and fasten them together, either by applying glue or hammering in metal pins or thin iron nails—the leather crafter's sewing pins. For the latter method, drive the nails through some of the holes you have marked, but not all the way through—just enough to hold the two pieces together. If necessary, you can pull the nails out again, using pliers or your fingers, if they interfere with your sewing. You can simply pull the metal pins out by hand.

First, match the two ends to be sewn together by cutting out the pieces and laying them one atop the other to fit. Then mark the desired line for the seam and use a stitching groover to cut out a small groove in which the thread can disappear. This way, nothing sticks out and the thread cannot become frayed. Then mark the space intervals for the individual stitches. It's useful to coordinate the intervals between the stitches and the distance between the seam and the edge, along with the thickness of the thread, all with each other. The distance between the seam and the edge should amount to at least one to one and a half times the thickness of the leather. Thus, if the leather is 4 mm (0.16 inches) thick, the distance between the seam and the edge should be 4–6 mm (0.16–0.25 inches). The interval between the stitches should be one and a half times the simple thickness of the leather. Therefore, it would be 6 mm (0.25 inches) in this case. For thin leather, you may have to plan for longer intervals so that you do not get too close to the edge. Extremely thin leather should not be sewn using the saddle stitch but rather using an industrial sewing machine, which is something not dealt with in this book. Over time, you will get an eye for what will be durable and what has a good and balanced appearance.

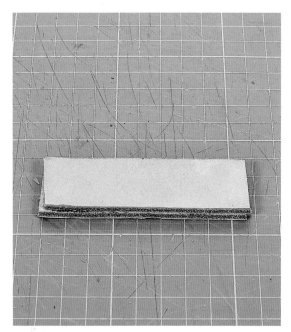

For practice, it helps to glue the two pieces of leather to-gether.

First, cut the decorative groove.

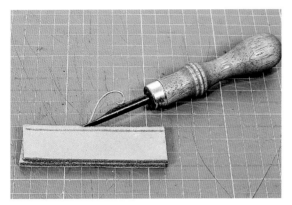

Bevel the edges on both sides (see p. 10).

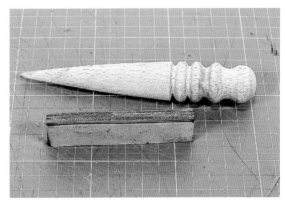

Use the wooden leather burnisher to round and smooth the edge.

Use the stitching groover to cut a groove for the seam.

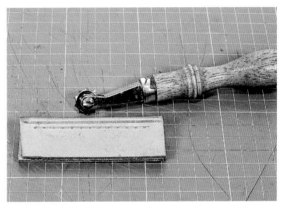

Use an overstitch wheel or wing divider to mark the interval between the stitches.

Clamp the piece in the stitching pony so that you are working toward yourself and the front side is to the right. This guarantees that you can always cut the groove from the good side. For sewing, you need a diamond awl that you can use with your right hand if you are right-handed.

Pierce the first hole, holding the awl so that the two cutting edges are at two and eight o'clock when you are looking at the piece from the right side. Piercing the leather at a slant ensures that, on the one hand, the two threads will stay in the seam better and more neatly, and, on the other hand, the leather is weakened as little as possible. If you were to pierce the holes parallel to the edge, the holes would quickly develop into a continuous weak area along which the leather can tear.

As soon as the first hole is pierced, insert a needle through it and pull on both sides so that the free ends are of the same length. Then comes the second hole, and now you begin to sew: Pierce the hole and keep holding both needles, each in one hand, meanwhile holding an awl in your right hand. Then stick the left needle through the hole from left to right until ⅔ of it is poking out of the right side. Place the right needle crosswise under the left needle from below. Pull both needles to the right and turn your hand so that you can stick the right needle through the hole. At the same time, you have to pull the thread coming from the left toward you, so that the thread from the right comes to lie behind it. This is the only way that you will achieve a slightly slanted, stepped fit of the seams.

Pull the two threads tight and you can move on to the next hole.

Clamp the piece in the stitching pony for sewing.

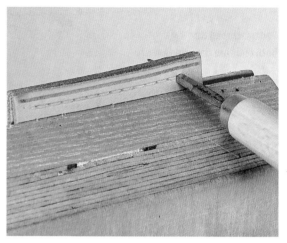

Pierce the first hole into the part of the piece that is farthest away from you—you are working toward yourself.

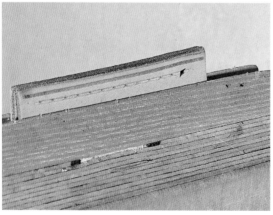

Pierce the hole at a 45-degree angle; if you are looking at the visible side of the piece, the two end points are at two and eight o'clock.

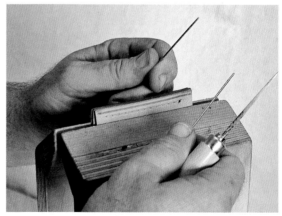

Hold the awl and one needle in your right hand and the other needle in your left hand; you will always keep the awl in your hand while sewing.

Pull the thread through the first hole, making sure that both ends are the same length.

Use the awl to prepunch the second hole.

First stick the left needle through the hole until ²/₃ of it is poking out on the right side.

Place the needle you are holding in your right hand under the left needle at a right angle.

This is the way you pull the left needle all the way through the leather.

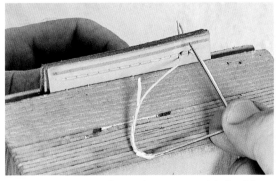

Now turn the two needles so that you can stick the right needle through the same hole.

Insert the needle behind the first thread, as seen from your perspective. This is important to maintain the stepped pattern you want.

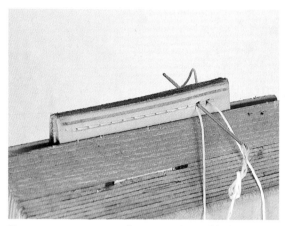

Here you can get an overview to see the position of the threads.

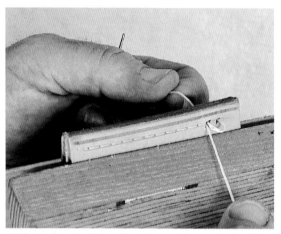

Pull both threads tight and make sure they are in the right position.

Pierce the next hole and continue to work your way forward.

As you get closer to the end of the seam, pierce the second- and third-to-last holes a little larger, because you will sew back over the seam, and here you must make space not just for two threads, but instead for four threads. To finish the seam, sew to the end and replace the diamond awl with the round awl. Use the round awl to widen the last hole but one and sew back over two stitches. It is necessary to use the round awl because you might cut the thread already in that hole if you were using a diamond awl. Now you can trim off both threads flush—don't worry; nothing will unravel. Finally, you can either tap the seam flat, using a cobbler's hammer with a polished hammer face, or press it into the cut groove, using the bone folder or wooden leather burnisher.

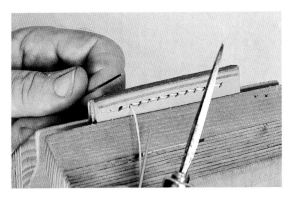

Pierce the next-to-last hole and the hole before it a little larger, because here you have to thread through four threads instead of two threads to finish the seam.

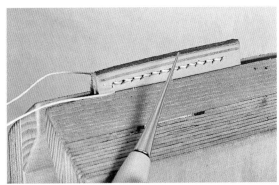

To finally sew back over the two stitches, switch to a round awl so that you don't cut through the thread.

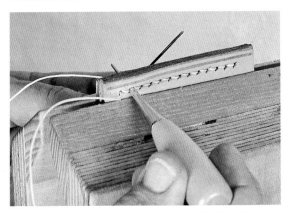

Pierce through the hole, but not through the thread.

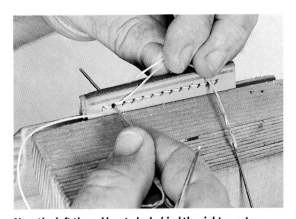

Now the left thread has to be behind the right one, to maintain the stepped pattern.

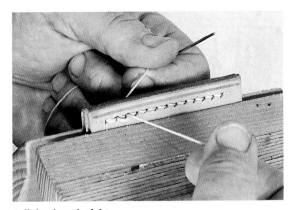

Pull the threads tight . . .

. . . and cut them off flush—the seam is finished.

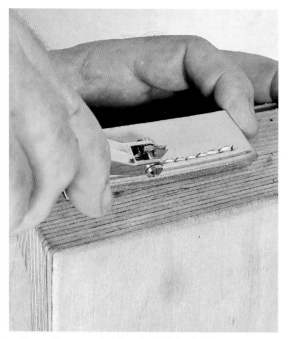

Roll over the seam with the overstitch wheel, so you recess the thread and make the intervals even.

The seam also looks neat and accurate from the back.

Baseball Seam—Butt-Stitch or Sew Two Pieces of Leather Edge to Edge

There are two fundamentally different ways to butt-stitch leather, which means sewing two pieces of leather together edge to edge. In one version, you use a round awl to pierce through the surface of one piece of leather, and as you do so, try to have it come out in the groove of the other piece of leather. Then you use semicircular needles to sew. This version requires very thick leather and a lot of practice.

The second possibility is the so-called baseball seam. Typical examples are the eponymous baseball, but this stitch is also used to make covers for car steering wheels or tool handles. It is much easier to do than the previous work method. To

make a baseball seam, first pierce all the holes, which is easy to do by hand with the leather still lying flat. Then sew using two needles and a lot of thread: Start at one end and each time stick a needle through, from the outside toward the inside, and pull both threads so they are the same length. Pass the needles from the inside toward the outside, so you are working crosswise. Work back between the two abutted edges; the threads will then lie between the two abutted edges. Keep working this way. Finally, once again pierce directly into the opposite hole and knot the threads on the inner side.

Match the leather to the object that you are going to cover.

Mark the distance to the edge and the interval between the stitches.

Clamp the leather in the stitching pony.

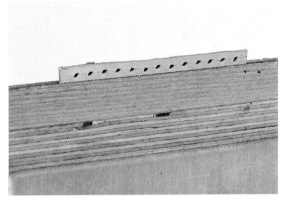

Prepunch all the holes; you will not be able to get to these places later.

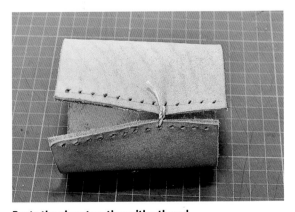

Baste the piece together with a thread.

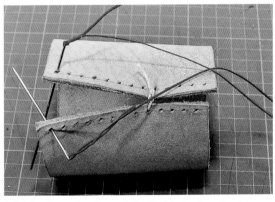

Stick both needles through the first holes from front to back.

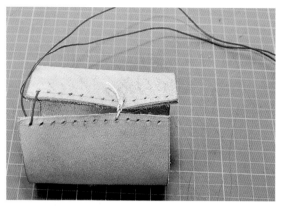

Both ends of the thread should be the same length.

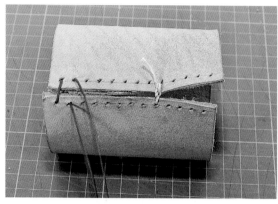

Cross the threads over and, coming from the inside, stick the needles through the second pair of holes.

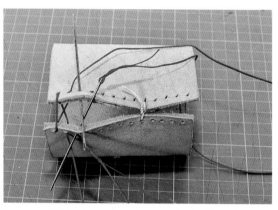

On every stitch, you are coming from the inside and sticking the needles toward the outside.

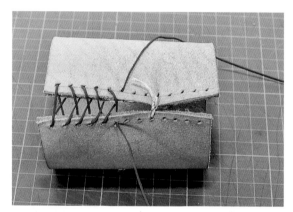

Do not pull the stitches too tight, so that you will be able to keep some freedom of movement.

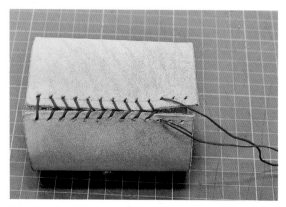

Shortly before the end, pull the stitches tight; tweezers or needle-nose pliers are helpful for this.

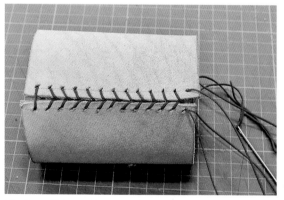

Finally, pull the entire seam tight and even out the abutted edges.

To finish the seam, stick the needle through from the out-side inward.

For the finish, knot the two threads together on the inside.

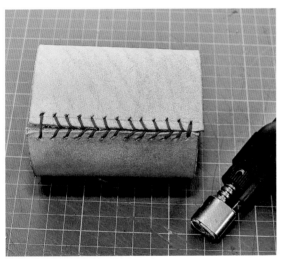

On the inside, fuse the two ends of the threads.

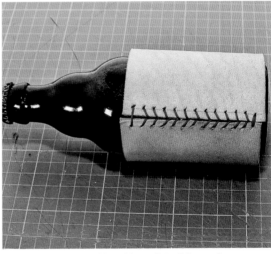

Trying it on and checking the quality of the work

Working with this version also lets you sew things that you would otherwise not be able to work on from the inside. In such a case, first sew from a distance, using a very long thread, and then draw the stitches together in the second step by gradually pulling the thread tight until the seam has closed up. Knot the end. Finally, you should burnish the seam with a bone folder or wooden leather burn-isher, particularly if it is supported by an object inside.

Sewing Chamois Leather

Tanning chamois, which involves only applying oil and a lot of mechanical manipulation of the hide, is the oldest method for finishing leather. You will need a round awl, a needle, and thread. In the completely classic mode, sinews are used to sew chamois leather, and you work with needles and awls made of bone. Most projects made of chamois leather are sewn with the inside out and then turned right side out, so that there is no visible seam on the outside and there is no need to burnish any edge. The holes are prepunched with a round awl, because this way the holes close again,

which would not happen with holes made using a diamond awl. When working with chamois leather, there is no way for you to sink the stitches of a seam or cut grooves into the edge, because this fleecy material will not work this way.

To sew it, simply hold the two parts that you are going to join together, or clamp them in a stitching pony and pierce the holes by eye. Then sew, using one thread and one needle, as shown in the fol-lowing pages. Make an especially big knot at the end of the thread so it cannot slip through the hole.

> **Note:**
> **Here we are using a red thread to make the work easier to see; using a sinew would be truer to the original methods.**

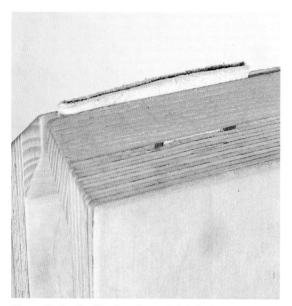

Clamp the leather firmly and very tightly in the stitching pony so that it cannot curl up.

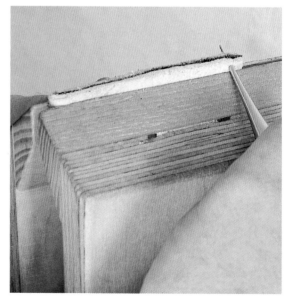

Pierce the hole, using the round awl.

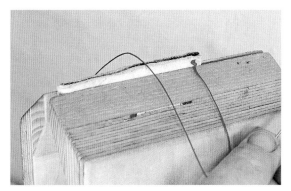

Stick the thread through the leather from right to left until the knot comes against the right side of the leather.

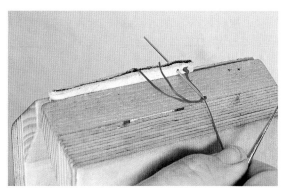

Pierce the next hole and pass the needle through the hole again from the right; the thread will then lie on top of the edge.

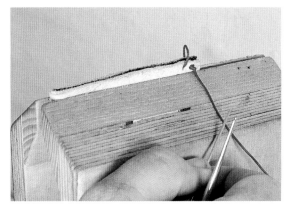

Pull the thread just tight enough that a small loop remains above the edge.

Stick the needle, facing away from you, through this loop.

Pass the thread through the thread loop and then pull it tight. By doing this, you are putting the pressure on the hole opposite, which makes sure that no unsightly wrinkles form on the thin leather.

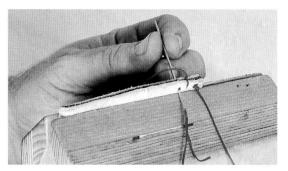

Now continue sewing, following this pattern.

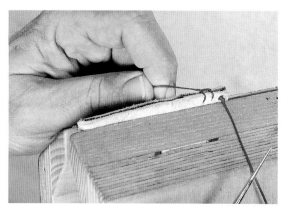

The thread should lie centered on top of the edge.

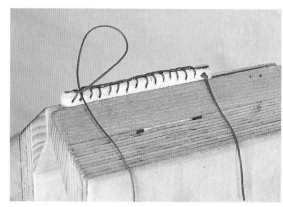

At the end, make an additional loop.

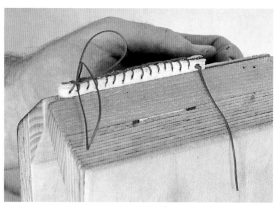

Pass the thread through this loop and tie a knot this way.

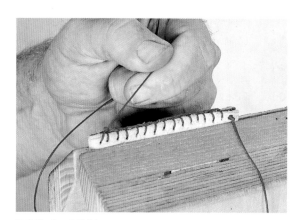

Pull the knot tight.

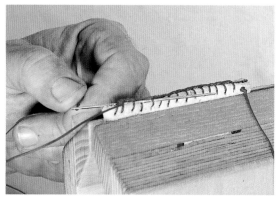

To make the stitches neater, stick the needle under some of the loops.

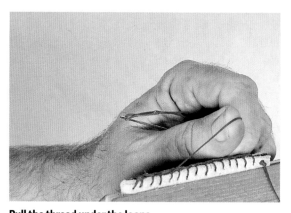

Pull the thread under the loops.

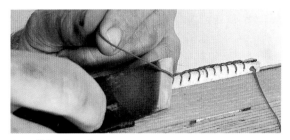

Cut off the thread.

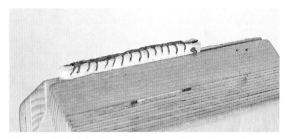

The seam is finished, but of course, with such supple material, it doesn't look as accurate as when you are using saddle leather.

On top of the edge, you can see the thread that prevents the seam from stretching.

After turning the piece right side out, you can see only the cross stitches.

Another possibility is to use so-called glover's needles, which have a three-cornered, sharp point. However, these are practical only when working with very thin leather, since they can penetrate thick leather only if you apply a lot of force. Use an artificial sinew for your stitching material. This is a synthetic thread with a shape that is broader and more flat than round. Cut the thread to a suitable length. Usually, this kind of thread is also too thick when it comes from the factory, but you can separate out individual strands and thus determine the thickness yourself. This thread is extremely durable, and you need only part of the sinew. To sew, hold the two sides of leather together and pierce through the leather directly with the needle. Then pass the thread over the edge to the other side and stick the needle through the leather again from the right. Now, don't simply pass the thread over the edge but, rather, pass it once through under the thread so that the thread lies on top of the seam and always runs down through the next hole at a right angle. This will give the seam additional strength and also ensures that it, and therefore the edge, won't get stretched out. Finally, you have to knot the thread and slide the free end under the thread loops for a few stitches and then cut it off. A thimble is a big help for sewing.

> **TIP:**
> **You can also use waxed dental floss instead of a sinew.**

Preparing and Manipulating the Leather

With its special structure and the different tanning methods, leather offers a wide range of options for preparation, manipulation, and decoration. From simply applying oils and waxes, to tooling and staining, to aging to wet molding and hardening, the possibilities are almost unlimited. Here you and your creativity can live it up.

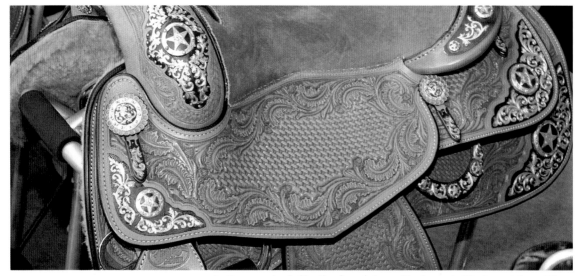

In Germany, tooled leather is mainly used to decorate Western-style saddlery.

Tooling

To decorate leather, you need to use vegetable-tanned or russet leather that is not oiled on the grain side. This vegetable-tanned leather is usually very light colored before it is treated in any way. Before tooling, you should moisten it with a sponge or a spray bottle, which makes it immediately turn darker. After a few minutes, the leather regains its original color and you can start on the tooling work. The simplest style is a basket weave pattern, for which you need only two stamping tools. The pattern conceals any scratches and spots on the piece of leather.

Using the tooling method to decorate leather is rather uncommon in Germany, but in the United States, you will find decorations in this style on almost every saddle, and tooling itself is a recognized art form.

What Will You Need?

Thanks to the internet, it is easy to purchase stamping tools or stamps for decorating leather. Again and again, you will find offers for leather-tooling sets including two dozen or more different stamping tools for what is really very little money. Here, how-ever, the devil is in the detail, because these sets are usually poorly made and leave only a poor-quality impression in the leather. That being said, you will never need all of the stamping tools in a set. All you need to get started is a border tool and a stamping tool for the basket weave pattern. I recommend tools by the Craftool company, but you can also use tools made by other well-known American manufacturers. The no-name products that you can get from a well-known, big US online mail order company, however, usually produce only poor impressions in the leather. Next, you still need a soft-faced hammer; it can be a wooden hammer or a mallet made of wood or plastic, and with this, your arsenal is already complete. In the beginning, you can improvise all the other tools, or you can rely on the tools you already have.

To do the tooling work, you need a solid, heavy base so that the underlay also forms a counter support, and you can see the stamping tool clearly (see "Stone Slab" on p. 7).

When tooling, bright, sufficiently intense, diffuse light is necessary. You should avoid cast shadows because they can quickly make you drop in the stamping tool the wrong way.

Before You Get Started

The old phrase "Less is more" applies to leather tooling because an excess usually looks bad. To ensure that the pattern works, you should keep it at sufficient distance from the edge and not overload the piece. Also, you should not start by tooling an entire saddle right away but, rather, start on a beer mat first. Or you can first familiarize yourself with the tools and the leather by using scraps. Note that tooling can stretch out long, straight pieces such as belts or hatbands. You should therefore plan the pattern so that you have the option of making the pieces shorter without destroying the entire project. For example, attach the buckle to a belt only after the tooling work is finished, so that you can shorten the belt beforehand. It is also a good idea to keep measuring long objects from time to time, so that, if necessary, you do not drop in the last stamps but stop earlier. The longer and more intensively you moisten the leather, the more its shape can be distorted. To prevent this, you can use a sponge or a spray bottle to moisten small areas and keep applying moisture while you work.

Another possibility for preventing a distorted shape is to fasten down the flesh side with tape. Duct tape works well for this. But you can also use packing tape that doesn't stretch.

WHAT DO YOU NEED?
- **Stamping tools**
- **Soft-faced hammer**
- **Sturdy base**
- **Diffuse light**

On the left piece, the tooling is far enough from the edge and small stamps were used, so it is possible to make enough impressions on this small piece of leather. The one on the right looks overloaded; the large flowers are difficult to align, the border tool used is too big, and the basket weave pattern doesn't come into its own because there is room for a maximum of only three stamps.

Basket Weave Pattern

You need only two stamps to create a basket weave pattern—one for the basket weave pattern itself and one for the border. Keep the line bordering the pattern on the piece at a sufficient distance from the edge. Tooling work is always done on flat pieces and never on the already sewn project. If possible, you should never tool a basket weave pattern straight along the piece edge, but always at a slight angle, unless you are making a wide belt or guitar strap. Otherwise, it looks better if you design it at a slight angle, from the bottom left to the top right. To achieve that, draw an oblique line across the greatest length of the piece to anchor your work. You drop in the first stamps along this line—always to the right and left of it, butting against the side of the previous stamp and overlapping it. Working this way, you will quickly fill the area with impressions. You can also tool the basket weave in a much denser pattern, so that the two sides completely overlap. This works well on smaller pieces, for example, and makes it easier to work cleanly, especially if you are a beginner.

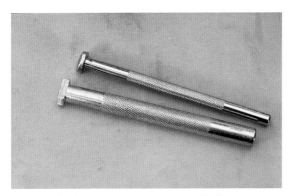

To make a basket weave pattern, you need only two stamping tools—a basket weave stamp and one for the border, a so-called border stamp.

First round off the corners and bevel the edges (see p. 10), then moisten the leather with a spray bottle and cut in a groove for decoration.

Draw the border for the pattern with a wing divider; here it is about half an inch or 13 mm.

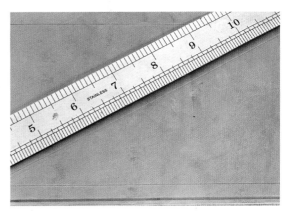

Use a ruler to mark where the pattern will run, here from bottom left to top right.

First, work your way along the anchor line. As soon as this is done, stamp in the next row, working along one side up to the edge, and then work on the other half. Always work nice and evenly; preferably, use three light strokes per stamp instead of one stroke that is too hard, because this damages the leather. As soon as you have filled in the area up to the border with full stamp impressions, drop the stamp in at the edge so that the shaft, which you are holding at an angle, produces only a partial impression. You can use this method to stamp the pattern along the border.

> **NOTE:**
> For the sake of the photos, the anchor lines have been cut much deeper than you normally would on real pieces. Normally, it's enough to be able to see the lines. As soon as a patina is applied, they will be clearly highlighted again.

33

The first stamp on the anchor line, not too close to the border.

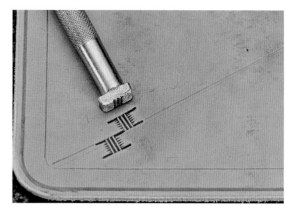

The second stamp overlaps the first one along the anchor line.

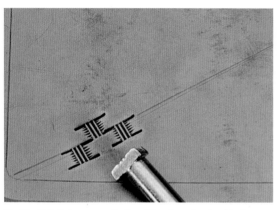

For the third stamp, again drop the stamping tool below the anchor line, overlapping the second one.

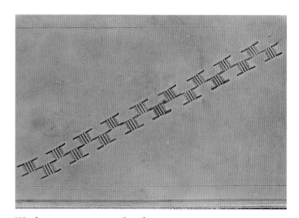

Work your way across the piece once.

Now drop in half a stamp toward the border, tilting the tool slightly.

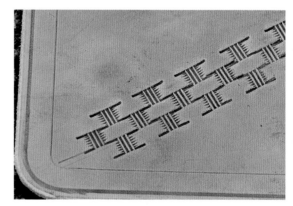

Abut the next row from below.

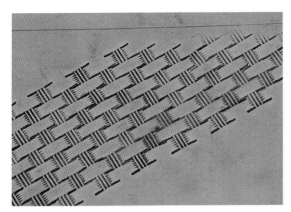

After a few rows, the impression of a basket weave pattern emerges.

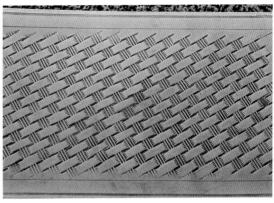

First fill in the middle area; leave the border empty for the time being.

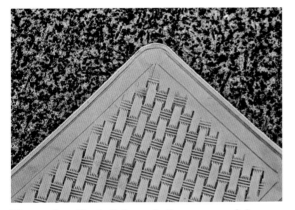

Then work making half stamps in the corners and along the edge.

Keep in mind that you will still finish the pattern off with a border tool, so you don't have to work your way to the line bordering the pattern everywhere.

Use the border stamp to give the border a clean finish and to make the stamps that were struck fully disappear visually. This tool, also known as a border tool, is used to visually conceal any uneven area along the edge. These tools are usually semicircular, and you hammer them in with the straight side toward the edge. A basket weave pattern looks more professional when it is finished off with a border stamp than it does without it. To make sure the border stamps also fit cleanly together, you have to watch out when you come to the end of the line. It will be particularly noticeable if the last stamp doesn't quite fit in or if it comes out with a large gap at the end. To prevent this, you need to be particularly careful when making the last four to five stamps: If there is room for only about five stamps on your piece, then hammer one in right in the corner at the end of the line—I like to turn the stamping tool around here so that the semicircle fills the corner in exactly—and fill the space in between by eye, without hammering the stamps in. To do this, just press the stamps in very lightly by hand so that you can just barely see the impression. Feel free to leave some space between the individual impressions, because if you distribute the available space among three or four intervals here, it will be less noticeable than if half a stamp is missing at the end. The corners always catch your eye, and therefore, irregularities are more noticeable here than in the middle of a longer line. As soon as you are satisfied with the layout, you can finally hammer in the stamps. After this, the piece of leather has to slowly dry out, and then you can sew your piece.

To tool the edges, first drop the stamping tools in each corner and continue working from there.

When there is space for only four to five stamps to the corner, tool them in by hand as a test to check how they fit.

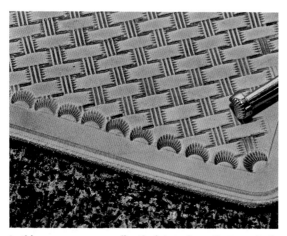

In this way you can equalize the intervals, so that you don't end up lacking space for half a stamp width at the end, something you can't conceal at a corner.

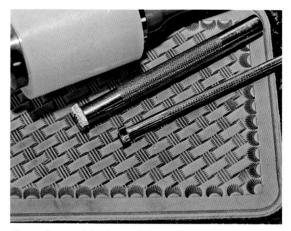

The tooling work is already finished on the piece.

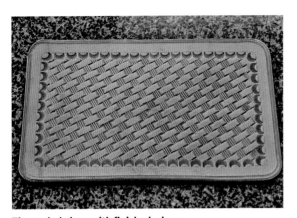

The tooled piece with finished edges

To make the pattern really come into its own and to make minor imperfections disappear visually, you can give the leather a patina by applying an antique stain, here in a tan color.

Tri-Weave Pattern

To tool a larger area, making a simple weave pattern by using a tri-weave stamping tool works very well. You will find such a stamp with the designation "X503S." The advantage of this stamp is that there are raised "pins" in the corners, which make it easier to abut it to the previously stamped impression. You only have to abut the stamp to the previous stamp, and the pins slip automatically into the already existing holes in a way you can easily feel. This pattern works particularly well for round pieces such as coasters because it looks the same from every direction.

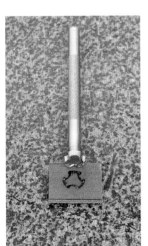

Left: Single stamp

Right: The tri-weave pattern works especially well on round pieces such as these coasters.

Square Weave Pattern

Square weave patterns also lend themselves well to stamping larger areas. When using these patterns, however, you have to be careful that the stamps don't get off center, because this is particularly noticeable with this pattern. It works very well on rectangular or square pieces. Since the impression from the stamping tool is relatively large, the piece should also be relatively large, to let the pattern come into its own.

The square-weave pattern is hard to align properly.

Barbed-Wire Pattern

Stamping tools that look like barbed wire are popular for creating a border. However, these patterns are used only by themselves; they are not suitable, for example, for finishing off a basket weave pattern. The do work very well for decorating a book cover, a bracelet, a belt, or a briefcase, and if you imprint your initials in Western-style script in a corner, this makes a simple and stylish way to enhance the piece. Barbed-wire stamping tools come in a set of four; each set includes a stamp with a design of twisted wire, a stamp of wire with two and four barbs each, and one of wire turning a corner. When tooling, make sure that the fine wires line up with each other perfectly. Also, this pattern tends to get off center quickly and then looks like bad workman-ship. But if you approach the tooling work calmly and pay attention to the following things, then, in fact, it isn't that difficult: First, draw an anchor line on the leather, positioning the tool above the line, because right in the middle you won't be able to distinguish it well enough to be able to work. Thus, the anchor line will then lie below the wire

and has to be offset downward a bit; otherwise, the wire will not be positioned in the middle on a bracelet, for example.

Let's start with the simplest thing, the stamping tool with the twisted wire. Here it is important that you apply the two stamps so they are aligned exactly, and then strike them only lightly. The tool was designed so that you can set it back half a tool width and thus conceal the transition. With a little feeling, you will notice how the stamp slips into the impressions that have already been made; then, another light strike and the transition is perfect.

The stamps with the barbs should be hammered in at an interval equal to three to four of the wire stamps. With the barb tools, it's especially tricky to abut the stamping tool exactly to the already struck impressions. Good light, a sense of proportion, and your anchor line will help, however. Here, too, it is advisable to first press in the stamp lightly and then carefully tilt it backward, without changing its position, in order to check the pattern. If everything matches up, tilt the stamp back down and hammer it in; if not, you can correct the positioning and, after you hit it hard, the impression left by your first attempt will no longer be visible. Barbed-wire stamping tools are used either to make a straight line or a frame on a rectangular piece. The reasons for this are design related, because you can't use it to create arcs. Instead, you can make the design branch off at a right angle only by using the corner tool. When it comes to corners, a sense of proportion is again required, because you can hammer in this transition cleanly only at the end of a piece of wire. If the interval doesn't fit when you do this, then you can drop in the piece of wire stamp so that it overlaps halfway, and then you must drop in the corner stamp just where the wire ends. Therefore, it is best to always place the end of the straight piece where it doesn't really matter. When making a book cover, for example, this would be in the direction of the spine, since the distance toward the lateral edge should be even at the top and bottom.

Barbed-wire stamping tools are available in a set of four, which you can combine as desired.

Rope Tool

A rope tool is a single stamp that you can simply drop in, one after the other, to create the appearance of a twisted rope. This decoration can also stand on its own and also tends to get off-centered easily.

You can apply the stamp along a flat line to suggest a narrow rope, or position it upright to create a wider line. The pattern looks especially good if you leave a little space between the individual stamp impressions. However, this requires a lot of practice and a sense of proportion and is therefore more something for the advanced leather worker.

You should not stamp the corners too close together, so that the impression of a rope is retained.

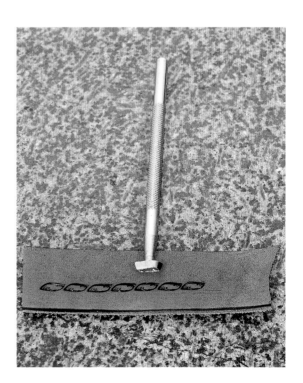

Rope pattern

Meander. The top row shows two individual stamps on the left.

Meander Tool

The meander tool looks simple, but you can create impressive patterns with it. There are a few things you need to keep in mind here so that the pattern ultimately looks really good. For one thing, you should pay careful attention to staying on the border line, because that is where you can immediately see any irregularities. It is helpful if you precut the line using a knife, because then the stamp will cut the leather down there cleanly and the finish appears even. Otherwise, it should be remembered that this pattern isn't so much a matter of the leather material that will be cut out, but rather much more a matter of the wavy line that it leaves behind. You should also make sure that the individual stamp impressions abut each other directly and don't overlap, because then the wavy line will be too narrow.

To do the tooling, stamp the two lines on the leather—they must be laid out exactly parallel—and trim them as needed. Moisten the leather and work along one line first. When this is complete, the opposite one follows. Working this way lets you position the stamp better. The pattern is relatively wide, and you should therefore apply it sparingly. If you want to combine the pattern with other tooling patterns, such as a basket weave pattern, then the piece should be at least A4 size. This is the only way to show both the meander on the one hand and the filled area on the other to their best advantage; the filling will then also be finished off using a border tool. Do not overload your piece; the eye of the beholder always needs areas that make an impact by themselves.

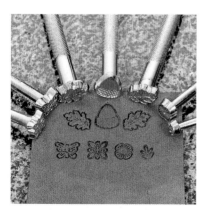

Individual stamping tools that can work when used all by themselves

Figure Stamping Tools

Figure stamping tools are individual stamps that display flowers, leaves, or animal heads, for example. You should use these sparingly because they make a better impact if they are used to decorate only a few areas of a piece. For example, a figure stamp of oak leaves and acorns fits into a corner of a book cover on a book about hunting. If, on the other hand, you were to decorate a belt with one and the same horse's head along its entire length, then your piece would look rather childish.

Since figure stamps are a bit more expensive, you may quickly become inclined to use them on every piece. But that doesn't create a particularly professional effect either.

Two complete alphabet sets in different sizes and fonts

Alphabet

There is a wide selection of stamps of the letters of the alphabet, which you can use to personalize your pieces. Since you will usually use only initials or nicknames, ornate capital letters are sufficient and even prettier than a standard font, which is actually used only to designate models, for example. Before buying, you should think about the height you want the letters to be. They should be around 12–15 mm (0.5–0.6 inches) high, because initials that are too small will not look right. Most alphabet sets consist of the stamping plates and an interchangeable T-slot holder. To align the letters cleanly, you should clamp a wooden ruler to the piece so that all the letters are at the same height. Do not clamp the ruler so tightly that it leaves marks on the damp leather. Now all you have to do is align the letter spacing so that it is pleasing to the eye. At the same time, you should pay attention that, for example, the capital "I" is much narrower than a "W" or an "R." That is why the "I" must be set farther apart from the other letters than the square plate provides. If you simply set the letters next to each other so that the plates touch, the spaces can be unsightly. Therefore, you should strike in the first letter and press the next one in only lightly with your hand, so that you can just recognize the impression. Check if the spacing works this way, and then set the letter on the impression and strike it in. This may sound a bit complicated and pedantic perhaps, but it makes a lot of difference in terms of the visual effect and ultimately creates the difference between amateur and professional work. Alternatively, you can sand the plate of the "I" to size on the side, so that the space corresponds to what you want.

Left: Aligned lettering with narrow spacing between the individual letters.
Right: The effect of lettering when the plates are set side by side—the visual impact of the spacing is too large.

> **NOTE:**
> Remember that nobody will be looking at your pattern with a magnifying glass, but always from some distance. Small irregularities therefore will not be apparent to the eye. The rest will come with practice.

Treating the Surface

Leather is a natural product that reacts to sunlight, dirt, and sweat, among other things—so it needs protection. This is already partially provided during tanning and finishing for oil-tanned leather. Other types of leather, such as leather intended for tooling, are deliberately not given protection. It is precisely this kind of leather that needs to be protected by applying the missing oil or wax afterward, so that it will no longer absorb water and it cannot become stained.

To select the right care product for your piece, you need to know how these products work. There are leather oils that are also applied during tanning and impregnate the leather. Water can no longer penetrate wherever the oil has been absorbed, because water and oil cannot mix due to their chemical composition. In addition to the protective effect, the oil also makes the leather soft and pliable. This is desirable for some types of leather and applications, but for some other ones, more of a disadvantage. For example, a knife sheath or a pistol holster must be hard and able to hold its own. A dog leash, on the other hand, should be soft and pliable. So if you should happen to use leather that hasn't already been oiled or waxed to make a dog leash, then you have to add it in the form of leather oil. The ideal way to protect a leather holster against water stains and environmental effects is to apply a mixture of leather oil and wax. Such products are made by practically melting the fat and wax together to make the wax easier to apply. In this process, the oil penetrates into the upper layers of the leather and leaves the wax behind on the surface, where it forms a thin, water-repellent protective layer without making the leather too soft or making it lose its stiffness.

Here you can see the different degrees that the color changes due to the application of different leather care products.

Neatsfoot oil is a typical kind of leather oil and was originally extracted from calf's foot bones. The oil stored in the foot bone has a particularly low melting point and becomes liquid at room temperature. It penetrates the natural leather material well and harmonizes with it.

When using care products that should protect the leather but maintain its stiffness, you should make sure that they contain a high proportion of beeswax. Warming it up helps the leather absorb the product better.

For all types of leather preservatives, you should take note that these products can change the color of the leather. Leather oils usually make it darker than beeswax-based products will. You should first make a test by applying the preservative of your choice to a remnant of leather. This way you won't experience any nasty surprises and you won't be disappointed by the color and effect.

Dyeing

There are several methods you can use to dye leather. Most available leather dyes are water-based stains and are intended for unoiled vegetable-tanned leather. They penetrate the dry leather and dye it thoroughly. This has no effect on the various features of the leather, and it can still be oiled or waxed later on.

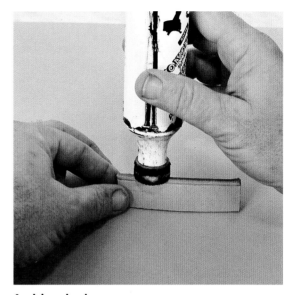

1. Leather patina or antique finish; 2. leather stains; 3. edge dyes

Applying edge dye

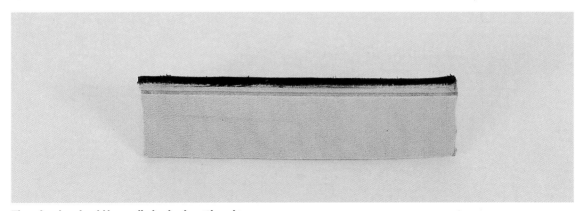

The edge dye should be applied only along the edge.

Left: two different color tones created using leather stains; *right:* a piece of antiqued or "patinated" leather

Stain can also be used to highlight tooling work. There are special stains for this, which are primarily intended for patinating, as the artificial aging of leather is called. In the process, the deeper areas become darker and the upper ones lighter, giving the impression of leather that has been used for a long time. These stains are made in gel form, so that you can apply the stain thickly by using a sponge and then wipe it off. In this way, you will give the deeper parts of the pattern a more intense and darker color, and the parts above will remain lighter. There are all sorts of transitional colors in between. The staining creates more depth and a reinforced 3-D effect. Finally, you have to let the piece dry and treat the surface.

For oiled leather, there are leather dyes that are applied as a layer of dye on the leather, like applying a coat of paint on a nonabsorbent surface. These colors rub off, and the plain leather emerges again. A stain, on the other hand, is absorbed into the leather and may in some circumstances even color it all the way through, depending on how much is used and how long the stain is allowed to penetrate.

Leather dye, a piece of sponge, and the leather

Wear gloves when you apply the dye.

Wet Molding

Wet molding is a particularly interesting method of working with leather. The leather is soaked in lukewarm water until no more bubbles form. When the leather is saturated, it can be easily molded into shape. Leather used for wet molding should not be oiled, so that it can absorb the water—vegetable-tanned leather is preferable. For wet molding, you can either make molds or shape the leather by hand. Making molds is an advantage if you want to produce several identical pieces. A mold consists of a lower part, over which the leather is laid, and an upper part, which presses the leather onto the lower mold and holds it in place as long as necessary until it has become dry enough to hold its shape.

Freehand molding is used, for example, for making knife sheaths and handgun holsters to improve the fit. To do this, wrap the handgun or knife in cling film and stick it in the soaked sheath or in the holster and press the leather firmly against the object. Let the piece dry this way, along with the object. Wet molding gives the leather additional strength or stiffness. Finally, you should protect the outer surface by using wax-based care products.

The wet molding technique is used for making a knife sheath, where a precise fit is important.

Hardening

Hardening leather works in a way very similar to wet molding. It is used, for example, to make armor out of leather in the live-action role-playing (LARP for short) and cosplay "scenes." But the leather used in the canteen project (see p. 98) is also hardened. There are several methods to do this. The quickest way is to soak the unoiled vegetable-tanned leather in hot water at 80°C, until it is soft. Take it out immediately and mold it into the desired shape. Then it just needs to cool and dry out. At the same time, the water must never be any hotter than this; otherwise the piece will become so hard that it breaks. In any case, be sure to practice on snippets of the same piece of leather beforehand until you get a feel for the molding process.

Hardening Dragon Scales to Make LARP Scale Armor

You can use hot water for hardening; 80°C is ideal, but you should not let it exceed this temperature.

Put the piece in the hot water and wait until no more bubbles rise to the surface. The piece has become saturated and has assumed the temperature.

Carefully remove the piece, using a pair of tweezers.

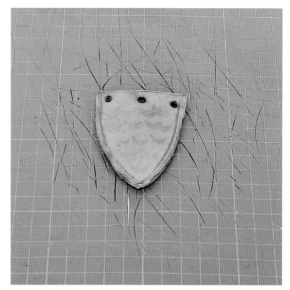

Bend the piece into shape and let it slowly dry and cool down. When it has been treated with a little leather care product, the dragon scale is then ready for you to continue working.

The second, better option is to harden unoiled, vegetable-tanned leather, using beeswax (see p. 106 and following on this). To do this, warm the leather in the oven to 80°C and the beeswax in a saucepan to around 80°C. With the wax, a few degrees of difference won't matter, but it should not boil. Now brush the leather with plenty of wax on all sides and put it back in the oven for a few minutes until it has absorbed the wax. A piece of baking paper under the leather keeps the beeswax from dripping into the oven. Spread liquid wax on the leather again and repeat the process as many times as needed, until it will no longer absorb any wax. Mold the still-warm leather into the desired shape. When it has cooled down, it retains its shape and is as hard as wood and water repellent. You should note that the leather will darken a lot when it is hardened using wax—a test on a remnant of leather is recommended. Finally, the only thing left to do is to burnish the surface with a soft cloth.

Setting Rivets

It may be necessary to set rivets if a point is inaccessible or a project doesn't allow for a sufficiently long seam. In the past, sewing was the preferred method in leather crafting, because rivets were expensive and labor was cheap. Today, it is the other way around, and many things are simply "nailed together" with rivets—also because today, there are only a few who know how to appreciate a good seam. If you want to / must set rivets, it is best to use copper rivets with burrs.

To set these rivets correctly, you need a "rivet setter." This is a special tool that is quite inexpensive and indispensable for this kind of work. The rivets have a broad, flat head and a shank. First, punch a hole of the appropriate diameter for the rivet. Use a rivet to fasten the pieces of leather that you want to rivet together; to do this, the copper head should be on the visible surface. Then slide the burr onto the rivet shank and, as you do so, notice that the burr doesn't seem to fit. But that's intentional, because now you will use the rivet setter. There are two holes on this tool; now, the deep hole is what you need. Slide it over the rivet shank and place the head of the rivet on a clean, smooth surface. Strike the rivet setter, using light, well-measured blows. The burr will move down the rivet shank and clamp down—that's exactly what is intended. The two pieces of leather are pressed together and the burr is fastened in place.

Use a pair of pincer pliers or a hacksaw to cut off the rivet shank, leaving a stump of 1–2 mm (0.04–0.08 inches). Now you need the semicircular indentation in the rivet setter: Place this over the rivet shank and strike the rivet setter using light, measured blows. This will make the end of the rivet form into a "mushroom" so that the burr cannot come loose again. This calls for taking a cautious approach, because if you try to shape the end with just one strong blow, then it may happen that the rivet will snap and damage the leather.

Copper flathead rivets are a little more complex to set but hold better than double rivets.

Stick the shank of the rivet through the hole.

Put the burr on; it will get stuck because the hole is a bit too small.

Use the rivet setter to strike the burr toward the leather until it is clamped lightly in place.

Snip off the shank so that that 1–2 mm (0.04–0.08 inches) remain.

You can also sand down the rivet cleanly; then the rivet head will look better afterward.

You can rivet the shank by using the rivet setter or, as shown here, with several light blows of a hammer.

The rivet head should be hammered out into a mushroom shape; then it will hold securely.

I don't want to hide the fact that there are also other rivets available. For example, there are some made from brass that have two parts, a top and a bottom cap, which are hammered together. These rivets have become the rivet of choice in the industry nowadays and hold very well. I don't like them because you cannot adjust them in terms of the thickness of the leather. You always need to have the right length of rivet because you can compensate by only a millimeter. Besides that, you cannot fasten two pieces of leather temporarily; instead, this can be done only when the rivet caps are hammered together. These so-called tubular rivets come with a tool in every package; you should use it to protect the domed rivet cap on the visible side. Therefore, you can't just knock these rivets together on an anvil just like that, because this would flatten out the cap and it will no longer look good.

Beginner Projects

W e will begin with simple projects for beginners. To start, I will show only a few methods, but these are ones that you will need for many projects. You can, for example, practice how to burnish the edge of a bracelet before you try it on an entire belt. Some of the projects can also be completed without making a seam, which reduces the number of tools you require and should quickly lead to your first sense of achievement.

Bracelets

Materials:
Leather straps 20–50 mm (0.8–2 inches) wide—as long as the circumference of your wrist—+ 2 cm (0.78 inches) of vegetable-tanned or oil-tanned leather
1–2 snap fasteners
Leather dye of your choice

Tools:
Half-round / English point strap end punch or cutter
Wooden leather creaser
Wooden leather burnisher
Edge beveler
Edge dye of your choice
Stamping tool of your choice

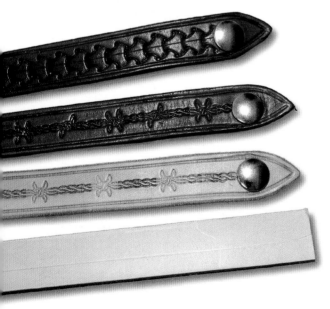

In my courses on sewing leather, I always start with a bracelet, because making them is the best way to demonstrate and re-create the most important steps you use in working with leather, such as finishing edges and treating surfaces. If the bracelet is to be fastened with a snap, it is not even necessary to make a seam. The starting material is a leather strap, which should be 2 cm (0.78 inches) longer than the circumference of your wrist. This way, you will have enough material available to cut it to size. Due to the snap fastener and the thickness of the leather, it can be difficult to take an exact measurement, and the bracelet will then be too tight. To get the most accurate measurement, wrap the raw leather strap around your wrist and mark the length by making an impression with your thumbnail.

The width of the bracelet depends on personal taste. I prefer a width of 20–25 mm (0.78–1 inch). Bracelets 40 mm (1.5 inches) or wider will quickly look very martial. But you can also trim the leather to 50 mm (2 inches), dye it black, and set two snap fasteners next to each other, and in this way make a heavy metal, rock, or Goth fan happy. When treating the surface, however, make sure that you do not use agents that contain too much oil, so that your clothes won't get greasy spots.

Once the length is established and you have shaped the two ends—either using a half-round or English point punch, just as you like it—you have to use the wooden leather creaser to cut a decorative groove line and bevel the edges. Then finish the leather edges with a leather burnisher so that they come out nice and round and there are no leather fibers sticking out. You can now also dye the edges with edge dye. Simple tooling with such designs as barbed wire or meanders also works well on bracelets. If the bracelet is wide enough, add initials and it will make a beautiful and individual gift.

When choosing the snap fasteners, it is important that the snap shank is long enough and matches the thickness of the leather. In a pinch, you might have to remove some material on the leather flesh side or use other snap fasteners.

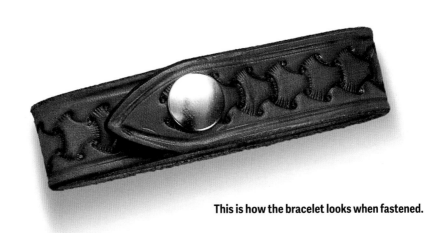

This is how the bracelet looks when fastened.

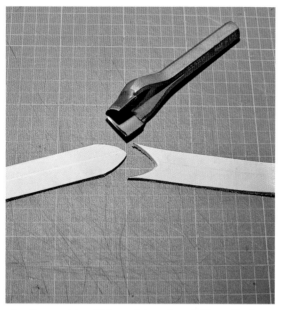

1 You can trim off the ends by using a knife or clip them off using a strap end punch; the strap shown here is 22 mm or ⅞ inches wide.

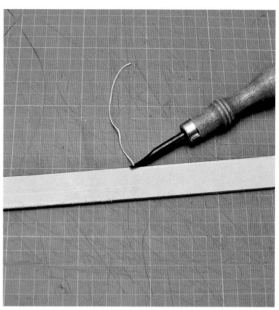

2 Use the edge beveler to bevel the edges along all sides.

3 Now use a wooden leather creaser to make a groove for decoration.

4 Use a spray bottle to first moisten the grain side of the leather; this will help you cut the groove more easily and let you make it deeper.

5 Start by using only a little pressure and cut short sections until you have cut the complete groove.

6 Round off the edge with the wooden leather burnisher or the folder; here again, start by using only a little pressure and then burnishing faster and faster.

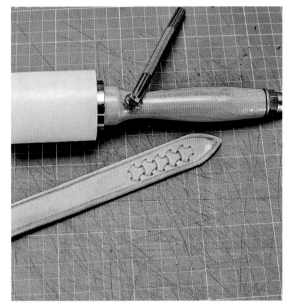

7 It is easy to stamp on the already moistened leather.

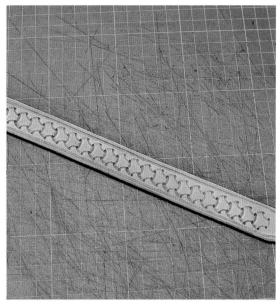

8 Keep stamping almost to the end; this will then be covered by the snap fastener.

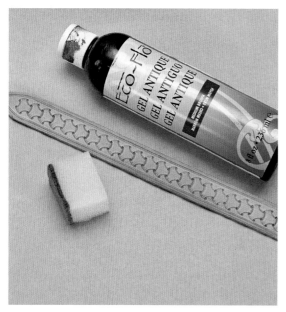

9 To give the leather a patina, you can use Gel Antique and a piece of sponge.

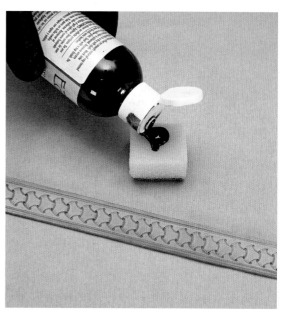

10 Put plenty of gel on the sponge and wear disposable gloves and use a sheet of coated paper as a disposable pad.

11 Spread plenty of gel on the piece, using circular movements; be careful not to dye the underside.

12 Here you can see that the gel hasn't penetrated to the deeper areas yet—you should go over these areas again.

13 Wipe the surface with a kitchen towel; the gel remains in the indentations and creates a dark contrast.

14 The bracelet finished with a patina. The tooling shows up well and looks three-dimensional.

15 Use a brush to apply an oil-based surface sealant, to also penetrate into the indentations.

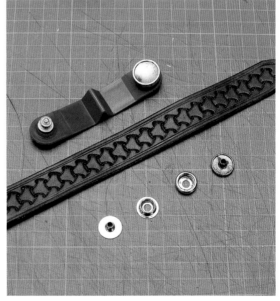

16 Finally, insert the snap fasteners.

17 The best method is to use punch pliers, because they work better than the punch supplied with the snap fasteners.

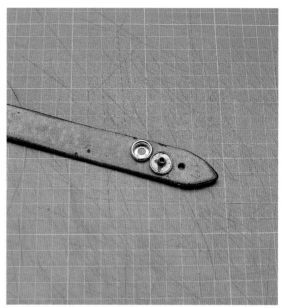

18 The part visible from the outside is the semicircular head; the catch with the spring is part of this.

19 Use the supplied tool to insert it.

20 This way, the round head of the snap fastener will not be damaged.

21 Place the lower part on a flat surface and rivet on the base, using one part of the tool.

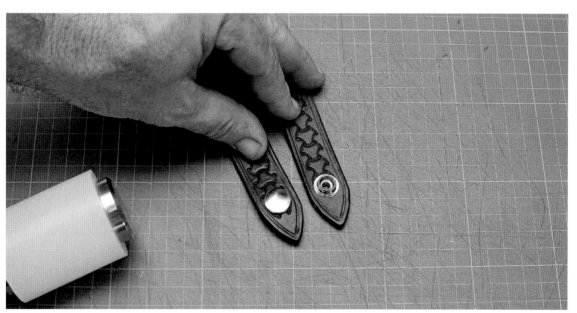

22 Both snap fasteners have been inserted.

Leather Apron

Materials:
Chrome-tanned leather or velour furniture leather
Leather straps
6 snap hooks
Grommets
Rivets

Tools:
Scissors
Rivet setter
Grommet setter
Wooden leather creaser
Edge beveler
Wooden leather burnisher
Punch pliers

Everyone knows the aprons you wear when barbecuing and cooking, featuring more or less funny sayings and printing. But aprons can also make a more serious impression and, above all, have more style. Leather aprons are a must near the barbecue, because the thick leather protects you from radiant heat and sparks. But it can also make sense to wear a thick leather apron when doing handicraft work.

When you buy an apron off the rack, usually it is not made of good leather, and often the straps were not attached properly—you can do all this better by making it yourself. Of course, before making it, you need to know what you actually want from the apron. I would like to give you some food for thought in the following.

The Leather

Most aprons are made from chrome-tanned leather because it is inexpensive and has a soft and supple fall. Besides, it also has a sleek surface, which lets you quickly wipe off splashes and dirt.

Using a type that is vegetable-tanned with enough leather oil is even better because it usually doesn't have the unpleasant chemical smell that some kinds of chrome-tanned leather do. Furniture velour or a similar leather in dark colors and with scars, such as the kinds used to cover high-quality car seats or couches or chairs, works very well. You can then make the straps from light-colored saddle leather, which creates a nice contrast to the darker leather. Add hardware made of brass to that, and the apron becomes a decorative piece that you will enjoy wearing for years.

The best thing to do is to go to a leather dealer and get the feel of the leather there. If it's soft and supple, the surface is rustic, and your gut feeling tells you that this is an apron you'll want to handle for years to come, buy it. The surface and the way the leather falls are important, especially when you have large surface areas, like those on an apron. It certainly should not be rigid or stiff, because it will not become much softer and you feel like you're wearing a tank. Also make sure that the leather doesn't smell of chemicals or stain your hand when you rub it, because if the latter happens, it will also happen later and the leather will stain your clothes when sweat and humid heat are added to the mix.

Note:
Leather is also not particularly easy to clean. Over time, the apron will get scuff marks and become dirty and greasy. This is called a patina. Only high-quality leather develops a patina. An inferior one just looks shabby and unkempt.

Cutting It Out

Any matching older apron can serve well as a pattern, but the cut of an apron should depend not only on the wearer's figure, but also on what activity you will be doing when it is supposed to protect you. Many manufacturers do not make their aprons from one piece, so there is often a seam in the middle of the apron. Although this reduces the waste, it isn't very sexy and also shows the work wasn't well thought out. It is exactly the middle of the apron that will come under the greatest stress, and that is why a seam there is very annoying. But that is exactly the reason you should make the apron yourself: because you don't want to make any compromises.

The length of the apron is important, because if you like to wear clothes such as Bermuda shorts, you should choose a slightly shorter apron so that you can still see some of your pants leg from the front. Otherwise, it will give the impression that you are wearing only the apron and no pants. Bare legs peeking out from under an apron always look pretty strange.

> **NOTE ON A NATURAL EDGE:**
> **An apron will look especially rustic if you incorporate the uneven edge into the design and use it to create a natural finished look.**

An old apron can serve as a pattern.

Pockets

Although pockets are practical, you should wisely choose how many you will have and how you arrange them. Aprons you buy usually have a lot of pockets. A pocket at chest level is there to hold your cell phone and reading glasses, but the contents can quickly fall out if you bend far over. The pocket at belt buckle level is usually very large and bulges outward, which ensures that it can end up holding a lot of debris—if you are woodworking, sawdust or wood shavings will collect in this pocket. On leather aprons, the pockets are usually attached as patch pockets and are not very large. If you need more space, then you should consider detachable bellows pockets.

I find pockets on aprons rather annoying and therefore like to leave them off, because I believe that an apron is primarily to protect the wearer, and I carry everything else in the pockets on my other clothing.

If you decide to make a leather apron yourself, then you have certainly already worn one or another kind of apron and know what you will need and what you can dispense with. That's exactly the beauty of making it yourself. The result suits you and doesn't necessarily have to be something that a product designer came up with for a big company.

Depending on what you are going to use the apron for, too many pockets can be unnecessary or even annoying.

Towel Holder

On a BBQ apron, a holder for a towel is very practical, because you should always have a towel handy. If you use a fabric apron for cooking, you can tie the waist ties together in front of your body and tuck a long towel—a touchon, also known as a pot holder or "pit cloth"—under the strap.

A leather apron doesn't have ties that you can knot together at the front to tuck the towel over. You can attach a strap holder or a ring at any place where you find the towel convenient. I find leather towel holders are better because they will hold the towel more securely there than a larger, riveted ring will, but that's a matter of taste.

To make a leather towel holder, you need a leather strap, two rivets, and two washers made of leather; you can punch these out using a 22 mm diameter (1 inch) hole punch.

The Strap

You can wear the apron in different ways: A simple neck strap can be made quickly, in fact, but the heavy leather apron will then pull on your neck, and this makes it uncomfortable to wear. This works well enough on light fabric aprons, but for leather aprons, you should have shoulder straps that cross over behind your back. These distribute the weight of the apron well, but putting it on involves a lot of contortions. Here you can use a "Y" backstrap, which has a single backstrap attached to the waist strap with a loop.

You can determine the length of the straps in advance and thus dispense with having to have ways to adjust the straps. Please note, however, that you tend to wear lighter clothing in summer and thick jackets in winter, so it may be necessary to be able to lengthen the straps a little anyway.

For the waist ties, it's a good idea to just fasten them with a carabiner or snap hook, because it is difficult to thread the ties through a buckle behind your body with one hand and then also get the buckle tongue through the small holes.

You can then attach the strap adjuster on the other side. But you can do without the adjuster completely if you attach the snap hook with a knot like a saddle strap.

You can simply sew the straps right to the apron or rivet them in place, but I find that neither is an ideal solution, especially since furniture and saddle leathers won't sew together nicely. It is better to hammer high-quality grommets, with an inner diameter of at least 14 mm (0.5 inches), into the apron and to sew or rivet snap hooks to the ends of the straps, which you then hook into these grommets.

You can attach the straps in a way that is visually appealing and at the same time very practical, by using sewn-on snap hooks and high-quality grommets.

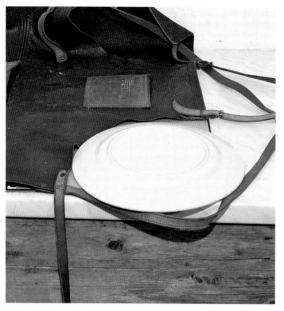

1 An old apron serves as a pattern; you can use a plate to help you sketch out the curves.

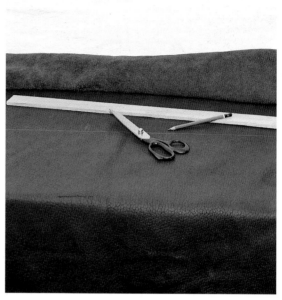

2 Mark where you will cut.

3 Cut the leather with scissors and not with a cutter; this is because the leather will otherwise pull on itself and the cuts won't be straight.

4 Make a cardboard pattern for the armholes.

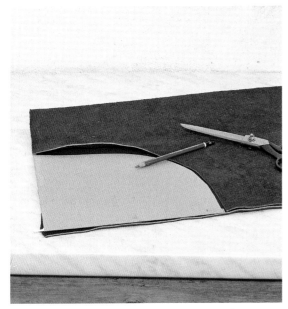

5 Lay the leather out doubled over and transfer one side to the other.

6 Round off the corners with a corner punch or the scissors.

7 To fasten on the straps, you need grommets and snap hooks.

8 Test the distance between the grommet and the edge on a leftover piece so that it is easy to hook the snap hook on.

9 Here, a cardboard pattern is used to make sure that the grommets are at an even distance from the edge.

10 Use the tool to set the grommets.

11 Now, only the straps still have to be riveted (see p. 47).

12 Use a lot of careful strokes to rivet the snap hooks into the straps.

Key Fobs

Materials:

Leather remnants, such as oil-tanned leather

Tools:

Depends on the type of key fob and how much effort you want to invest

Using remnants of leather is an ideal way to practice various sewing and leather working techniques, because they don't cost much and you cut them off anyway as you work. So that this leather does not end up as "valuable waste" and isn't used purely for practice, you can use it to make practical key fobs. This project is a very good one for beginners, and working on a key fob can also be a great activity for children.

You can learn a lot when making a key fob, and with just a little knowledge, you can make a presentable piece. And if it doesn't turn out well, not much damage has been done.

Key fobs that hang out over the top of your pants pocket—letting you pull your keys out without having to rummage in tight jeans pockets—are incredibly practical. It is easy to make such a simple key fob out of remnants of oil-tanned leather. These leather fobs are ideal for individual keys such as car keys; they shouldn't be attached to a heavy bunch of keys anyway, because the vibrations can cause the ignition lock to wear out.

Take a leather strap that fits comfortably through the hole in the key, and cut two lengthwise slits in the leather. First, loop one end through the first slit, then the second end through the second slit, and the key fob is finished.

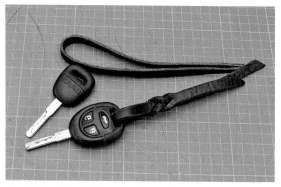

1 A simple key fob made of especially hard-wearing and pliable oil-tanned leather.

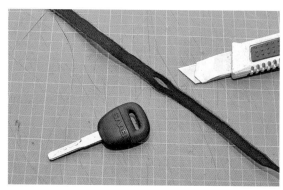

2 Use a cutter to slit the strap in two places.

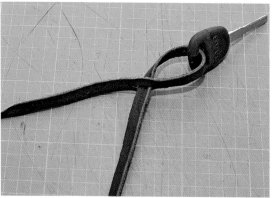

3 Pull the strap through the key so that both flesh sides of the leather are on top of each other, then insert one end through the slit in the opposite side.

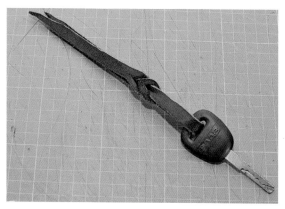

4 Then pull the second end through the other slit.

To make another simple version, cut out pieces of leather 2.5–3 cm (1–1.2 inches) wide and to the desired length. You can then tool them with initials or words such as "office," "barn," "safe," or "shed." Now punch a simple hole, pull the key fob through, and the project is finished.

You can also make these simple key fobs together with children; they would make a great project for a child's birthday party, adding the names of each child to their fobs. Depending on how long a name is, simply cut a piece from a belt blank and

bevel the edges with an edge beveler. Now you can make the fob even fancier: Moisten it with warm water, and tool on the name. Then use a wing divider to draw a border at an even distance from the edge, and stamp along it with a border tool. Now cut another decorative groove and burnish the edge. You can give the piece the final touch with black edge dye. Let the fob dry for a day and use a leather care product to restore some of the suppleness that the leather has lost due the water treatment and tooling.

1 To get a narrower end on the key fob, punch two larger holes in the leather to create a neat transition.

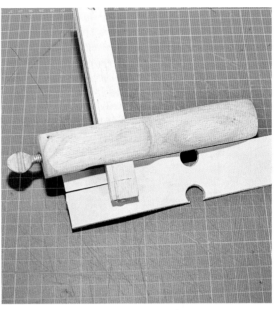

2 Using a strap cutter lets you work cleanly. Here, the leather is 1½ inch wide, and you should cut ½ inch off each side. You can also use a ruler and cutter.

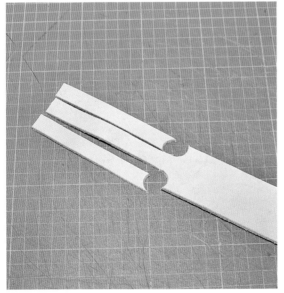

3 A ½-inch strip is left in the middle.

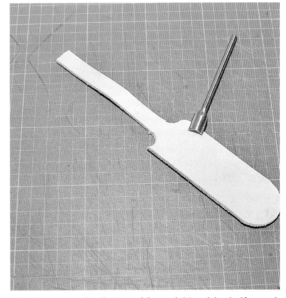

4 You can make the transition quickly with a half-round strap punch, but you can also work with a cutter.

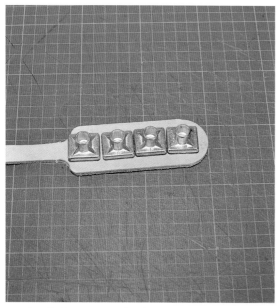

5 Set the letters on the leather and check that the piece of leather is big enough.

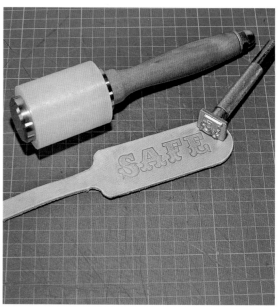

6 Bevel the edges and stamp in the lettering. Use another remnant of the same size to test whether the dimensions fit and the lettering is in the center.

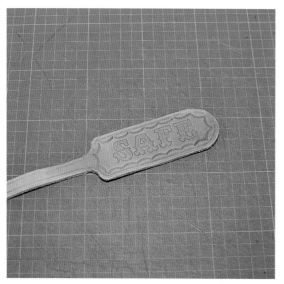

7 A simple border pattern and a decorative groove are quickly added; then you should finish the edges.

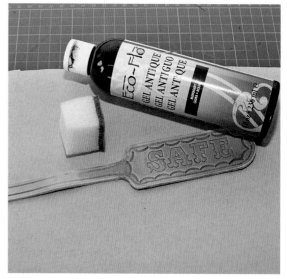

8 The best way to give the leather a patina is to use Gel Antique, here in mahogany.

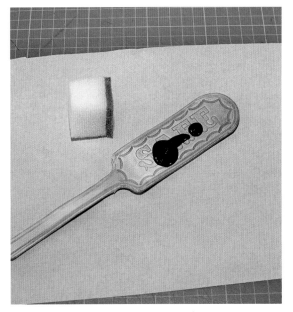

9 Pour a generous blob on the workpiece.

10 Rub the gel in with a sponge, using a circular motion, and check that it has penetrated into all the indentations.

11 Remove the excess gel with a paper towel.

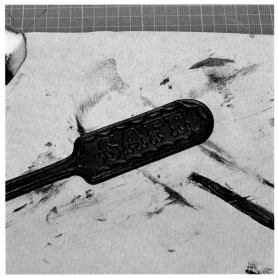

12 Dye the edges and the back also. A sheet of waterproof paper helps when doing this color-intensive work. After drying, apply oil or wax to the surface.

13 Turn the thin end over and punch two holes through both layers of leather.

14 Fasten the two ends together with a thin braided strap (see steps 15 and 16).

LOOPING

You can use thin braided straps to fasten two leather straps together. To do this, punch either two or four holes into the strap, depending on how wide it is.

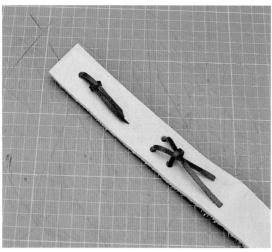

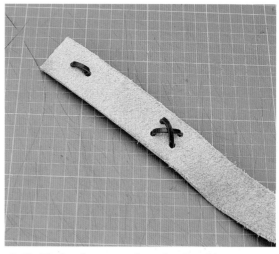

15 *Top,* the simple loops with two holes; *bottom,* with four holes

16 The looping as seen from the other side

If you want to invest a little more effort, cut out a fob as shown in the picture and rivet it to make a loop to hang the key ring.

Some sets of keys are simply too big to fit in your pants pocket, so a hand strap or even a neck strap can help. You can make this sample piece without any sewing or riveting. Of course, you can make short key fobs with a seam or use a real rivet instead of looping them.

The leather strip shouldn't be too thin, so that it also is comfortable to carry. About 15–20 mm (0.6–0.8 inches) is good; for ¾-inch snap hooks, you can rely on standard sizes.

You can also make longer key fobs to hang around your neck. For this version, however, note that the strap can easily come apart if it is pulled. To make it, attach a string or snap fastener to the key fob to make a predetermined breaking point so that you don't accidentally choke yourself with the strap hung around your neck if it gets caught on some-thing.

The loop at the end of this caretaker's key ring is fastened together with a braided strap.

From the side, you can see the structure of the loop.

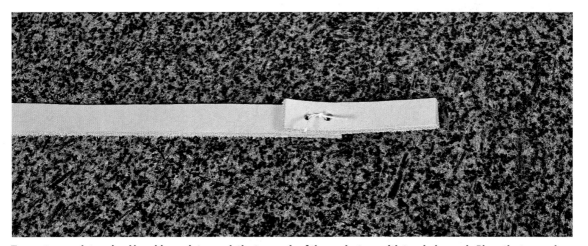

To create a predetermined breaking point, punch the two ends of the neck strap with two holes each. Place the two ends on top of each other and pull a thread through. Knot and trim the thread.

Intermediate Projects

• •

To make the following medium-level projects, you should already have mastered some of the simpler skills. You'll now add shorter and longer seams and simple tooling. However, the number of tools used in this chapter is still manageable, and thus the financial outlay is also kept within limits. But the pieces will be larger and so will the materials used. Nevertheless, the projects are easy for a technically skilled layperson to replicate, even if you will obviously need more time than a professional will. But the result will be something quite impressive.

Carrying Harness for an Axe

Materials:
2 14 mm (0.5 inch) leather straps
2 20 mm (0.8 inch) leather straps
1 halter square, two sided
1 20 mm (0.8 inch) harness buckle
2 roller buckles with 14 mm (0.5 inch) loop

Tools:

Cutting mat	Thread
Stone slab	Sewing pony
Knife	Awl
2 needles	
Wooden leather creaser and edge beveler	
Wooden leather burnisher and bone folder	

Any axe or hatchet that you can carry on your belt is, in my opinion, no more useful than a knife that you wear on your belt. If I take an axe with me, the handle should be at least as long as my forearm plus an outstretched hand; that is, about 50 cm (20 inches) long. When in the woods, I also prefer a light axe head with a long handle. No axe like this will fit on a belt.

Here, a sheath for the axe with a shoulder strap is ideal. You should design the harness so that you can take the sheath for the axe head out of the harness; this way, you can attach the axe to a backpack as required. You can then leave the harness at home, and the axe head is still always protected.

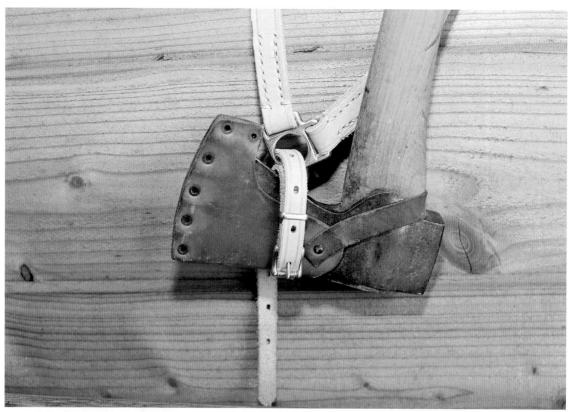

Fastening the axe head to the harness

Fastening the axe handle to the harness

TIP:
Be generous with the length of the harness so that you can wear it over thick winter clothing.

1 Materials for an axe carrier: two wide straps, two narrower straps, two roller buckles, a harness buckle, and a two-sided halter square

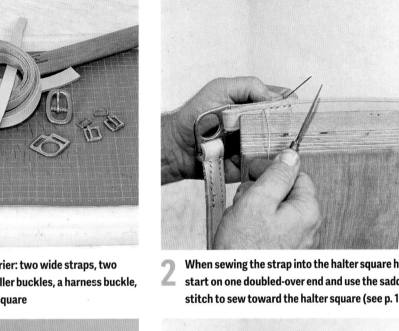

2 When sewing the strap into the halter square holes, start on one doubled-over end and use the saddle stitch to sew toward the halter square (see p. 18).

3 Stitching through the leather by the halter square can be difficult. Just hold it against the stitching pony from the other side with a cork.

4 To pull the two threads to the opposite edge to the second seam, pass both threads over the edge and insert the needles so that they come out in the middle, between the two layers of leather.

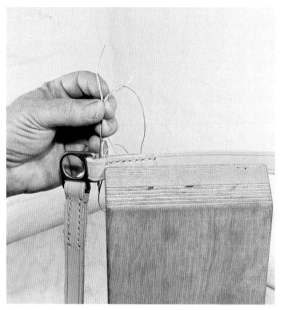

5 Guide the two needles through the leather layers to the other side.

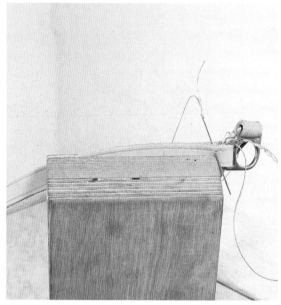

6 After reclamping, pierce the first hole and insert one needle at a time from the inside to the outside.

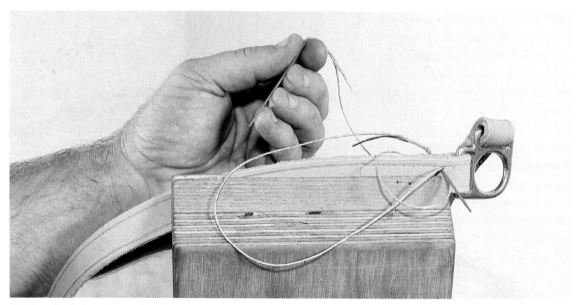

7 Pass both threads over the edge and through the hole again.

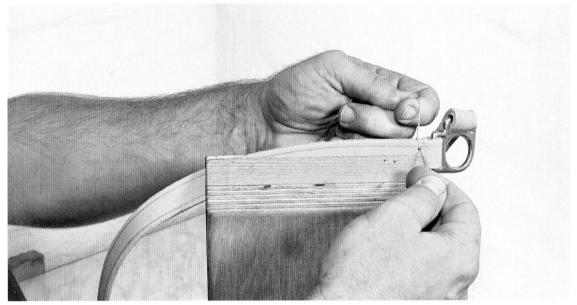

8 Pull the threads tight and continue sewing as usual.

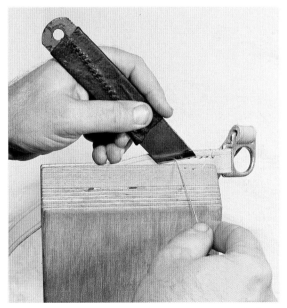

9 At the end of the seam, stitch back over two stitches and cut the thread off flush.

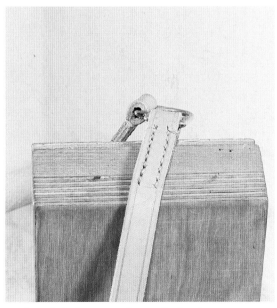

10 The halter square is sewn in cleanly.

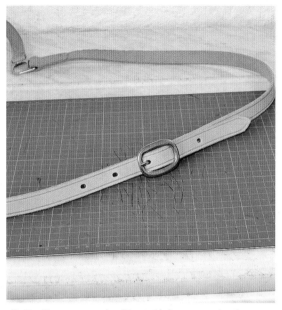

11 You can use a buckle at the front to make the strap longer or shorter.

12 Attach two straps and rivet the buckles in place—there is not enough space for a seam.

13 Unlike a belt, the strap has holes along its entire length so that your harness will be flexible.

14 The back is lined with a strap that is riveted at intervals . . .

15 ... so that the strap that holds the handle won't slip, and you can also fasten it to hang at different heights.

16 Make one side of the lower strap longer and rivet the halter square on so that you won't lose the strap.

Book Cover

Materials:
Vegetable-tanned leather, in 2 thicknesses

Tools:
Cutting mat
Knife
Awl
2 needles
Thread
Wooden leather creaser and edge beveler
Wooden leather burnisher and bone folder
Stitching pony

We know book covers mostly from our school-days. A leather book cover, however, will protect any much-used book, and it also makes it look good and can be customized. In the United States, book covers are often used for worn-out family Bibles, while in Germany, a cover is more commonly used to protect notebooks. For the latter books, the cover also makes it easy for you to keep small notes and business cards under the flap. For the design, especially for a hardcover book, keep in mind that the flaps into which you tuck the boards shouldn't be too close to the spine, so that it's easy to put the cover on.

The edges of the flaps on the book cover should be beveled and finished before it's sewn. Make sure, however, that you bevel the edges on the inner side that face the other side of the leather only where this part is exposed, because the edge should not be beveled under the seam.

Using initials or a design related to the book subject is a good idea for tooling the cover; you should tool them only in two corners diagonally opposite each other—because less is often more. Then add a simple border for decoration.

> **TIP:**
> The large surfaces and straight lines of a book cover are ideal for tooling, but at the very least, border design or initials work well.

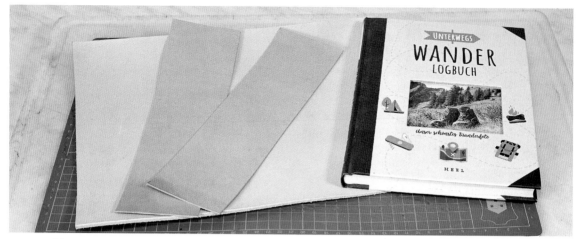

1 Roughly cut out three pieces of leather; the leather for the flaps should be significantly thinner than the outer cover.

2 The book itself serves as a pattern template.

3 The leather pieces for the flaps should be slightly larger than the outer cover, because everything will be glued together later and cut off flush.

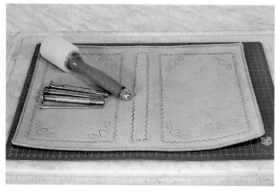

4 Tool the leather and cut the groove for recessing the seam and the holes for spacing the stitches.

5 After giving the leather a patina, continue by sewing on the flaps.

6 The flaps should protrude on three sides.

7 To make sewing easier, glue the flaps onto the large piece of leather.

8 Coat the surfaces to be glued with a leather glue and let it dry.

9 Place the pieces one atop the other and tap them into place with a clean, smooth hammer.

10 Trim off the thin leather for the flaps flush with the edge of the thick leather. Use the edge of the thick leather as a guide.

11 Clamp the book cover in a stitching pony and start sewing along the lower right edge.

12 Sew the long, straight seam with the saddle stitch (see p. 18) in one go; you will need a new piece of thread three to four times to do this.

13 Put the book in the cover to test it, and weigh it down overnight to smooth out the leather.

14 Bevel, stain, and burnish the edge.

15 A book cover made of leather is a work of art and protects at the same time.

16 The book can lie flat because of the weight of the leather.

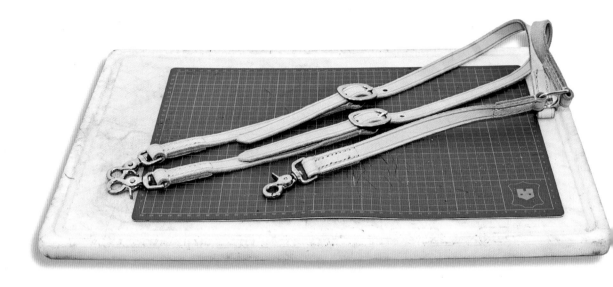

Suspenders

Materials:

Leather straps

3 swivel snap hooks

Ring or halter square with two sides

2 harness buckles

Tools:

Cutting mat

Knife

Awl

2 needles

Thread

Wooden leather creaser and edge beveler

Wooden leather burnisher and bone folder

Stitching pony

Suspenders are an expression of tradition and have become incredibly trendy again. Originally, they were purely for practical use; today, suspenders can be seen on catwalks and on many fashion magazine covers.

What could be better than to stand out from the crowd even more by wearing a handmade accessory? Suspenders not only offer a rustic touch but also bring real added value. On suspenders you wear on top of your clothing so they can be seen, it is essential to add buckles to adjust the straps, because this will add to the rustic look. On the other hand, if you have to wear your shirts over your pants instead of tucked inside and wear your suspenders under your shirt, you should take measurements beforehand and dispense with the bulky buckles.

The lower ends are equipped with swivel snap hooks that are hooked into the belt loops. This protects the belt or the pants, because the so-called alligator clips on commercially available suspenders must clamp very tightly or have serrated edges to hold the heavy pants securely. Beyond fashionable men's suits, only a few styles of trousers are still made with buttons for suspenders. These include such styles as leather trousers (Lederhosen) worn for hunting or the field uniform trousers of the German Armed Forces Bundeswehr. This version of suspenders with snap hooks has a decisive advantage: Whenever you might need to let your pants down, you have to open only three snap hooks and your suspenders stay under your outer clothing. If you are wearing this version, you don't have to take off any of your other clothes so you can slip off the suspenders. If you want to sew the suspenders yourself, then you should make them out of a backstrap and two shoulder straps. The straps are sewn together in a Y shape in the middle of the back or held together with a ring. The ends of the suspenders with the snap hooks can either be riveted or sewn; both styles have a rustic look— sewing, of course, takes more work. You can likewise either rivet or sew the separate straps with buckles to adjust the length of the suspenders. For adjusting the length, keep in mind that you should make a maximum of only five holes, as you would on a belt, and in the normal position, the buckle tongue should fit in the middle hole. Too many holes and ends that are too long always look bad, especially on custom-made items, and give the impression that you have just bought something off the rack. Therefore, instead of five, I punch only three holes, with the middle one defining the ideal length.

Taking Measurements

When measuring, it is important that you work as precisely as possible and first use a piece of string to make a pattern. You can then take the measurements and make a drawing or even a pattern. To sew on the buckles or snap hooks, you should calculate for another 6 cm (2.5 inches) on the actual piece of leather; 4 cm (1.5 inches) of this is for the seam, and you need the other 2 cm (1 inch) to give you enough length to the place where the strap is folded over and the buckle or snap hook is attached.

> **TIP:**
> To make the backpiece of leather, you should ask someone else to help you mark the angle; if you use a ring or ready-made metal part, everything will slip into place by itself.

> **TIP:**
> Do not apply too much oil or wax on leather that may come in contact with your clothing.

Sometimes—depending on the type of leather—the straps stretch during the first few weeks you wear the suspenders. You can tell that this happened because the strap has become a little thinner, and the elongated, unused hole is now longer than the other ones. However, usually the buckle will have already left ugly marks on the leather. If this happens, I would rather shorten the backpiece and sew it again or replace it completely, because that is less complicated and looks better than using the next hole.

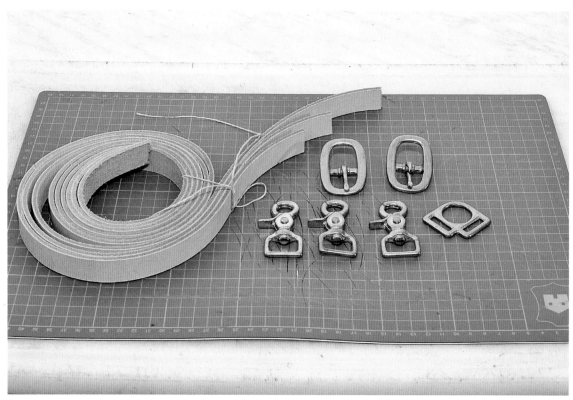

1 Materials to make a pair of suspenders: leather straps, a halter square with two sides, two harness buckles, and three swivel snap hooks.

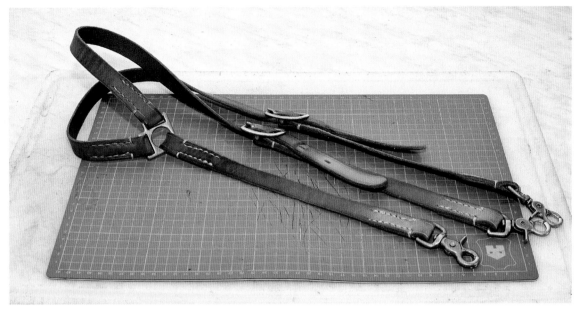

2 Use old suspenders as a pattern for the length.

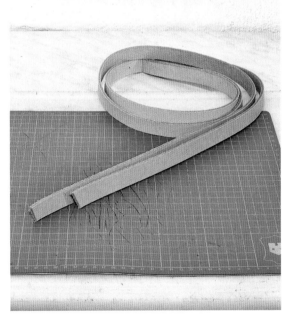

3 Stretch the straps out beforehand. Here, you can clearly see the difference between a stretched and nonstretched strap of the same initial length.

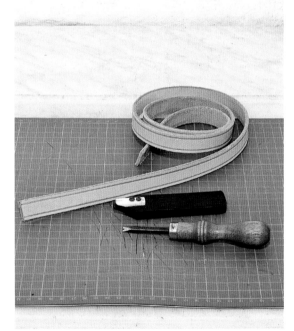

4 Cut a decorative line and bevel the edge of the leather.

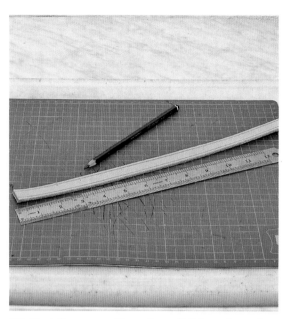

5 Mark the seams with a soft pencil; this can be easily removed with an eraser.

6 Cut a groove to recess the seam and mark the interval for the stitches.

7 First sew on the swivel snap hooks (for this, see steps 2–10, p. 77).

8 To make the slot for the buckle tongue, start punching at each end of the slot.

9 Connect the two holes and remove the leather in between.

10 Leave 2 inches of space for the buckle at the fold, so that it is easy to fasten.

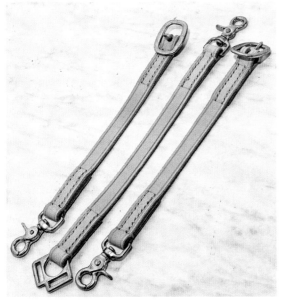

11 The three parts, with seams on each end. Next, sew the shoulder straps into the halter square (also see instructions starting on p. 77).

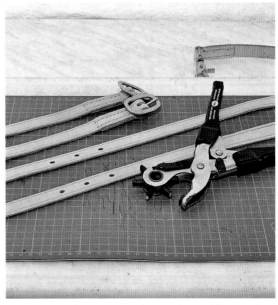

12 If possible, punch oval holes that are big enough into the shoulder straps.

Expert Projects

● ●

To work on the challenging projects in this chapter, you should already be able to sew a longer seam cleanly and evenly. You'll also need some tools that aren't in every toolbox. But on the whole, the projects aren't that much more difficult, although they are more extensive than the previous ones. They demand several hours of work and larger pieces of leather, which also makes them more expensive and makes any failure even more annoying.

Bottle Sleeve / Dice Cup

Materials:
Vegetable-tanned leather

Tools:
Cutting mat
Knife
Awl
2 needles
Thread
Wooden leather creaser and edge beveler
Wooden leather burnisher and bone folder
Stitching pony

In the United States, it is quite common for people to stick beverage cans or beer bottles into an insulated sleeve at a barbecue. Making a bottle sleeve like this of leather yourself gives the whole thing a lot more class and is something that you can customize wonderfully and give as a present. This is also a great way to create a dice cup, since the shape and the way it is made are identical. There are no limits to the imagination when it comes to designing the leather surface.

If you make the sleeve as a simple tube, then the project is quick and easy. It'll hold the bottle securely and firmly, and you have to make sure only that the bottle won't fall out of the bottom of the sleeve. You can prevent it from slipping out by gripping the sleeve firmly to hold the can or bottle in place.

You can also sew a bottom into the sleeve, but in fact, this doesn't always make the bottle completely secure, because you have to make the bottom to fit very precisely, but at least there is no way that the bottle or can would slip out. For a dice cup, you also need to make the latter version.

In this project, the two ends of the leather are butt-stitched together edge to edge; however, you can also use leather straps to make a piece of basketwork. It's important that you adjust the cutout leather to the bottle before sewing it, so that it'll fit

exactly later. As to the method of sewing, you can be quite flexible; there is a whole range of options, from using the baseball stitch to weaving leather straps together. Note, however, that certain techniques such as basket weaving will bulge up on the inside, and as a result, the sleeve may be too tight and the bottle will no longer fit inside. To make the dice cup, however, you can safely choose any way to join the pieces together.

TIP:
The large surface area of the bottle sleeve or dice cup is a perfect place for initials and basket weave pattern tooling.

1 Cut out two pieces of leather. The rectangular piece must fit snugly edge to edge around the bottles, and the round piece must match the circumference of the bottle bottom.

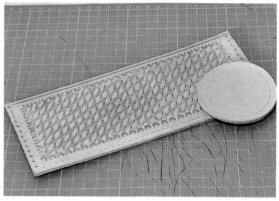

2 Finish the top of the large piece along the edges, and tool it to your taste. You should now pierce the holes for the baseball seam.

3 Apply a patina to the tooled piece and trim the edge of the round leather piece down to half its thickness.

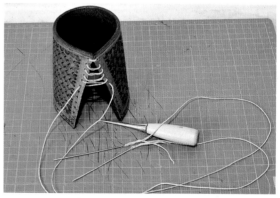

4 Sew the first piece together with a baseball seam (see p. 23).

5 To sew the bottom on, use the sharp awl to punch through the two layers of leather at an angle and continue working in saddle stitch (see p. 18).

6 The bottom now looks a bit strange and crooked and also bulges out; we will deal with this in the next step.

7 Soak the bottom in lukewarm water, push the bottom back in, and sand both rims smooth.

8 Now the bottle sleeve will be standing only on the rim; the bottom is curved inward and cannot tip over.

Waterproof Leather Canteen

Materials:

Vegetable-tanned leather
Turned wooden stopper
Some peas
Beeswax

Tools:

Cutting mat	Knife
Awl	Stitching pony
2 needles	Funnel
Wood to make the stopper	Hot plate and oven
Thread	
Wooden leather creaser and edge beveler	
Wooden leather burnisher and bone folder	

A bottle made of leather that is also waterproof? That works, and the sewing itself isn't even particularly challenging. All you need to use is a simple saddle stitch, which has already been described elsewhere (see p. 18). You can use a conical stopper to close it; you can either turn the stopper out of wood beforehand or buy one in the form of a cork.

In this project, the leather is by turns wet-molded, hardened, and soaked in beeswax, all of which again make it challenging. In earlier times, leather bottles were valued as unbreakable canteens, but they were also used as waterproof containers for gunpowder or other things that had to remain dry, such as salt or spices. During the Thirty Years' War, they were also widely used as bullet pouches, because the bottle's long neck would let the soldier pour out only a single bullet into his hand.

Vegetable-tanned leather is the only kind to use, because it works well for wet molding and hardening and will absorb the beeswax completely, which makes the bottle waterproof.

Pattern

The pattern is kept quite simple. You put two pieces of leather one atop the other and cut both out at the same time. This is simple when making a round object, but for a bottle with parallel, straight sides, the sides will tend to get drawn in at the middle after the wet molding, making the bottle look tapered. The pattern shown in step 1 is useful for making a canteen with a shoulder strap.

First, transfer the pattern onto the leather. In a pinch, you can draw it on two pieces of cardboard or on the plastic cover of a document folder and staple the pieces together with a stapler. This method lets you get a better estimate the size of the bottle neck, for example. Cut out the leather pieces, bevel the edges, mark the line for the seam, and cut a groove to recess it. Mark the interval between the holes and sew the two pieces of leather together firmly and cleanly, with the flesh side in. Hammer in the holes for the shoulder strap and burnish the edges all around. With this, most of the work has already been done.

> **NOTE:**
> **You should use a drill to drill through thicker layers of leather, because the conical shape of a hole punch would make the hole much wider at the top. Place a piece of soft wood underneath and carefully drill through the leather and another half inch into the wood, so that the leather doesn't tear.**

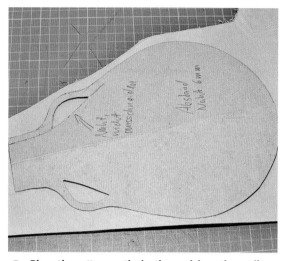

1 Place the pattern on the leather and draw the outline with a soft pencil.

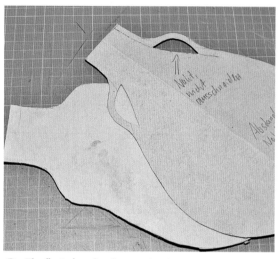

2 The first piece has been cut out.

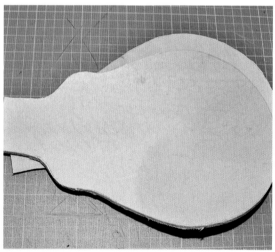

3 The two pieces here don't line up exactly, so they have to be reworked.

4 Make a groove 6 mm (0.25 inches) from the edge; mark the interval between the holes; glue the two pieces of leather together and trim both edges to fit. Then you can cut the groove on the other side to recess the seam.

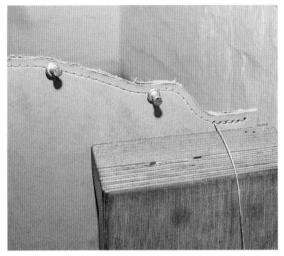

5 Sew the two leather pieces together with a saddle seam (see p. 18). To do this, use your smallest awl that will still go through the leather, so that you make the pierced holes as small as possible.

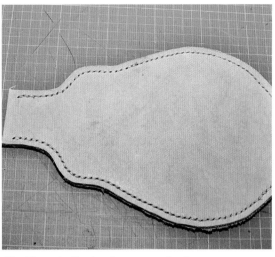

6 The outer line has been sewn cleanly.

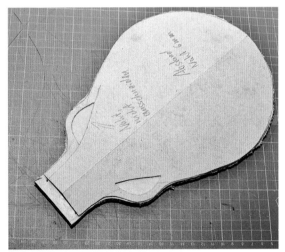

7 Use the template to mark the inner seams.

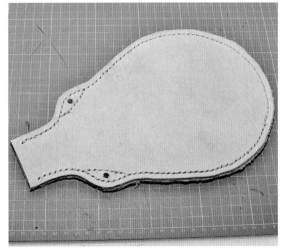

8 The inner seams are finished; now use a 6 mm (0.25 inch) drill to make the holes in the leather.

Wet Molding

Of course, a bottle still needs a certain internal volume. To achieve this, you must first soak the leather in lukewarm water until it is well saturated. First, use a pointed piece of wooden stick to widen the bottle neck and then use a wooden stick to separate the two leather sides.

Insert a funnel into the neck of the bottle and fill the cavity with dried peas or corn kernels. You can get popcorn kernels very cheaply in every supermarket, and dried peas are also available every-where. Always fill just a few spoonfuls of peas into the cavity and poke them in with the wooden stick. This way, you will gradually expand the bottle until you get the desired shape and volume. By then, the bottle should be full to the brim with the peas. Now insert the stopper and use it to shape the neck of the bottle.

Put the bottle aside, closed and filled with peas, and leave it at room temperature until the leather is completely dry. This way, the leather will dry out and harden. Under no circumstances should you try to speed up this process by leaving it at a temperature that is too high. If you let this happen, the leather would "burn" and not only become hard but also brittle or even shrink. As soon as the leather has completely dried out, you can remove the peas from the bottle. Use a flashlight to check whether you have actually gotten the last pea or kernel out of the bottle.

9 To make the bottle expand, you will need dried peas (or corn kernels), a funnel, and a stick to poke them in.

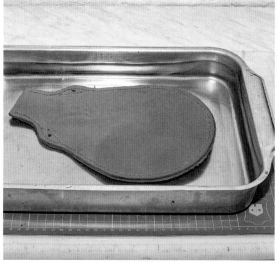

10 Put the piece in lukewarm water so that it can become saturated.

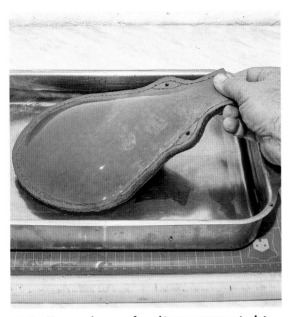

11 You can also use a funnel to pour some water into the bottle, so that it already will expand a bit and absorb the water well from the inside.

12 Insert a funnel in the bottle opening and pour in the peas.

13 Use the stick to poke the peas in firmly to make room for the next ones.

14 When the bottle is full to the neck and you can no longer get the stick in between the peas, close the bottle with the wooden stopper and let it dry slowly.

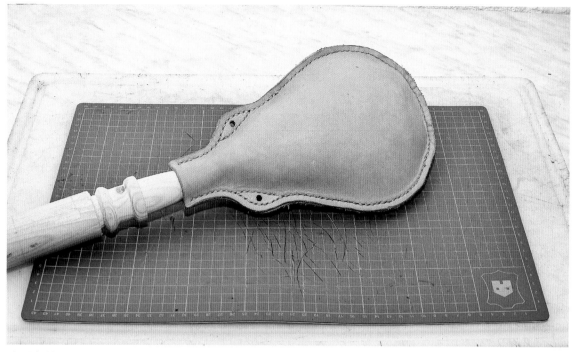

The dried bottle with the stopper, turned but still not cut down

The Stopper

If you want to turn a piece of wood to make the stopper, then you should choose wood that is as hard as possible and can be lathed and will polish well. While turning it, leave a long handle on the stopper and turn the end only when you are 100% satisfied with the way it fits. It is important that you select a very narrow angle and that you make sure that the stopper fits neatly all around on a surface as long as possible. This includes on the side with the seam.

Beeswax Treatment

Use beeswax to harden the material and make it waterproof. You can get the wax from any beekeeper who prepares it and offers it for sale. It is admittedly rather expensive, and you will also need at least 1 kilogram (2 pounds) so that you are able to work with it. In fact, you will need only a small part of this, but the larger the quantity you use, the more slowly it will cool and the easier it is to work with.

Liquid beeswax is as flammable as gasoline, and you should heat it only on an electric hotplate and not on a gas stove or even an alcohol burner.

To treat the inside of the bottle with the beeswax, first place it in the oven at 80°C until you can just touch the bottle with your hand. I like to use my dehydrator for this. In the meantime, you can warm up the wax in a saucepan; it should also not get hotter than 80°C (175°F). Pour the wax into the bottle through a funnel and swirl it around so that the wax reaches all parts of the inner sides. Then pour out the excess wax before it cools too much. Now put the bottle back in the oven for at least 10 minutes and keep the remaining wax in the pot at 80°C (175°F). Keep pouring new wax into the bottle and swirling it around. Pour the wax back into the pan and place the bottle back in the heat until the outside of the leather takes on a fatty-looking, darker shine. This is the sign that the wax has penetrated the full thickness of the leather.

Now you should treat the outside and especially the seams, applying the hot wax with a brush. Pour some wax into the bottle, insert the stopper, and turn the bottle upside down so that the wax also penetrates the seams around the stopper.

Finally, you should let the bottle dry out for a few days, then burnish it with a soft cloth and finally check for leaks.

A leather bottle like this is of course not as easy to care for as a plastic bottle, so you should empty it after each use, leave it open, and store it upside down so that it can dry out and does not get moldy.

If you want to be on the safe side, you can also use barrel pitch or brewer's pitch to impregnate the interior. This is a natural resin that is used to seal barrels.

Melt it in the same way you did the beeswax, and pour it into the warmed bottle. Swirl it around and pour out the excess pitch again. The pitch doesn't have to dry out, so it is enough to let it cool down. Then it becomes hard, waterproof, tasteless, and food-safe. However, you should not store spirits in the bottle for too long since the alcohol could dissolve some of the pitch.

NOTE:
Before showing someone a leather bottle like this, you should make it clear to them that they shouldn't squeeze it. This would splinter the sealing, making the bottle unusable, and you'd have to repeat the sealing process. Oddly enough, it seems that almost anyone who holds such a bottle in their hand the first time will squeeze it.

15 To saturate the bottle with beeswax, you need a funnel and a pot of beeswax.

16 Melt the wax to 80°C (175°F) and pour it into the prewarmed bottle.

17 Swirl the bottle around and pour the wax back out before it sets. Speed is of the essence here.

18 After a short time, the wax soaks through the leather and turns it dark.

19 For the second or third filling, put the stopper in the bottle and swirl it around so that the upper part is also "treated" with the wax.

20 After three to four passes, the bottle is almost completely saturated, and only the sewn areas have not yet been treated properly.

21 Warm the bottle and the wax again and brush wax on the areas not reached from the outside.

22 After one to two hours in a warm oven, the bottle is completely saturated. You can wipe off the outside and let the bottle cool.

Books and Websites

Das große Buch der Lederpfege (*The Big Book of Leather Care*)
Himer, Kim; Himer, Axel
Heel Verlag

Encyclopedia of Rawhide and Leather Braiding
Grant, Bruce
Cornell Maritime Press

Faszination Leder (*The Fascination of Leather*)
Fuchs, Karlheinz; Fuchs, Manuel; Derichs, Leo
Chimaira

Leather Braiding
Grant, Bruce
Cornell Maritime Press

Leatherworker.net (forum)
www.leatherworker.net

Leder brennen (*Leather Pyrography*)
Parsons, Michele Y.
Heel Verlag

Leder nähen (*Sewing Leather*)
Bothe, Carsten
Heel Verlag

Lederarbeiten (*Working with Leather*)
Gärtner, Michael
Heel Verlag

Lederinfo.de
www.leder-info.de

Lederlexikon (*Encyclopedia of Leather*)
www.lederpedia.de

Pro-Leder (*Pro-Leather*)
German trade magazine for the leather industry
www.pro-leder.de

The Art of Hand Sewing Leather
Stohlman, Al Tandy Leather Co.

The Leatherworking Handbook
Michael, Valerie Cassell

Manufacturers and Distributors

Bähr-Sattlerbedarf (Saddler's Supplies)
Eckeseyer Str. 52
58089 Hagen, Germany
www.sattlerbedarf-shop.de
Leather, rivets, needles, stamping tools, leather care products

Billys Westernshop
Caspar-Voght-Str. 42 20535
Hamburg, Germany
http: //www.billyswesternshop.de
Leather goods, jewelry, books, buckles

Carsten Bothe
Blumenstrasse 2
31167 Bockenem
www.carstenbothe.de
Leather-sewing courses

Der kleine Messerladen (The Little Knife Shop)
Allensteiner Str. 45
D-56566 Neuwied, Germany
www.der-kleine-messerladen.de
Leather, sewing thread and sinew, leather glue, leather finishing products, leather dye, snap hooks, rivets

Dictum GmbH
Gotlieb-Daimler-Straße
3 94447 Plattling, Germany
www.dictum.com
Leather care products, sewing, cutting, punching and stamping tools

Die Ledermacher (The Leather Makers)
Molkereistraße 8
86681 Fünfsteten, Germany
www.ledermacher.de
Leather, leather dyes, finishing and care products, stamping tools, books, courses

Dürnberger-Leder Punzier Laden (Dürnberger Leather Stamp Shop)
Dürnberg 1
83417 Kirchanschöring, Germany
www.die-duernberger.de
Leather, kits, stamping tools, leather dyes, care products, tools, patterns, rivets, courses

Heiko Kappey Sattlereibedarf + Lederhandel (Saddlery + Leather Supplier)
Achardstrasse 10
31319 Sehnde, Germany
www.kappey.de
Tools, leather care products, dyes, glue, leather, hardware

Jagdhundebedarf Falkenberg (Hunting Dog Supplies Falkenberg)
Rochusstr.
16 63457 Hanau, Germany
www.Jagdhundebedarf-falkenberg.de
Tools, materials and, above all, pieces, patches, and belt blanks

Langlauf Schuhbedarf GmbH (Shoe Supplies)
Am hohen Teich 11
44359 Dortmund, Germany
www.schuhbedarf.de
Glue, leather dyes and care products, tools, leather

Leather Stamps Tools
Sergey Neskromniy
Varna, Bulgaria
www.leatherstampstools.com
Tooling and stamping tools

Leder Baumann (Baumann's Leather)
Herzog-Wilhelm-Strasse 27
80331 Munich, Germany
www.leder-baumann.de
Leather

Leder und Sattlerbedarf (Leather and Saddler's Supplies)
www.ds-leder.de
Leather, stamping supplies, leather dyes, leather-finishing products, accessories, tools, pieces and patches, books, instructions, courses

Leder-Futzi (Futzi's Leather)
Kleine Bahnhofstraße 8 a
16356 Ahrnesfelde/OT Blumberg, Germany
www.lederfutzi.de
Leather dyes and care products from our own production
Made in Germany—leather dyes, leather care products, instructions

Lederhammer (The Leather Hammer)
Mühlstraße 64
64283 Darmstadt, Germany
www.lederhammer.de
Leather crafts and leather hobby products, stamping supplies, leather care products, tools, books

Lederhandlung Flach (Flach Leather Supplies)
Sternstr. 19/Hof
24103 Kiel, Germany
www.leder-fach.de
Leather, craft kits, and sewing accessories

Lederhaus Giese & Bruhm GmbH (Giese & Bruhm Leather Store)
Sonnenwall 69-70
47051 Duisburg, Germany
www.lederhaus.de
Leather, rivets, leather dyes, leather thread, accessories

Leder Hobby (Leather Hobby)
Seestrasse 103
13353 Berlin Wedding, Germany
www.leder-hobby.de
Leather, stamping supplies, leather dyes, finishing supplies, accessories, tools, kits, instructions, books, courses

Ledershop-Chiemgau (Chiemgau Leather Shop)
Marderweg 40d
86169 Augsburg, Germany
www.lederwerkzeugladen-chiemgau.de
Tooling stamps, stamping tools, leather dye, glue, finishing products, handicraft sets, templates, books

Lederversand Berlin (Berlin Leather Mail Order)
Krossener Str. 32
10245 Berlin, Germany
www.lederversand-berlin.de
Leather, care products, dyes, glue

Lederkram (Leather Stuff)
www.lederkram.de
Leather, stamping supplies, leather dyes, finishing products, accessories, tools, pieces and patches, instructions, and leather know-how

Lederzentrum GmbH (Leather Center)
Raifeisenstraße 1
37124 Rosdorf, Germany
www.lederzentrum.de
Leather dyes and care products

Miller Custom Leather & Tool Co.
1203 S 55th St.
Temple, TX 76504, USA
www.etsy.com/shop/Leather-Tools By Clay
Tools

Nordisches Handwerk (Nordic Crafts)
Carl-Gauß-Str. 3 b
D-23562 Lübeck, Germany
www.nordisches-handwerk.de
Leather, rivets, straps, rings

Rickert-Werkzeug (Rickert Tools)
Neunkirchener Strasse 56
91207 Lauf an der Pegnitz, Germany
www.rickert-werkzeug.de
Leather, stamping tools, 2-D and 3-D stamps, leather dye, glue and finishing products, tools, kits, instructions

Tandy Leather Factory, Inc.
1900 SE Loop 820
Fort Worth, TX 76140, USA
www. tandyleather. com
Leather, stamping supplies, leather dyes and finishing products, accessories, tools, craft kits, books, instructions

About the Author

Outdoor professional, hunter, and certified biologist Carsten Bothe lives and works as a freelance journalist in Lower Saxony, Germany. He has lived with trappers in the United States and gained his outdoor experience through hunting and exploration trips to the United States, Canada, and New Zealand.

https://www.carstenbothe.de/